Same - Different

🖍 the butterflies:  – yellow   – purple

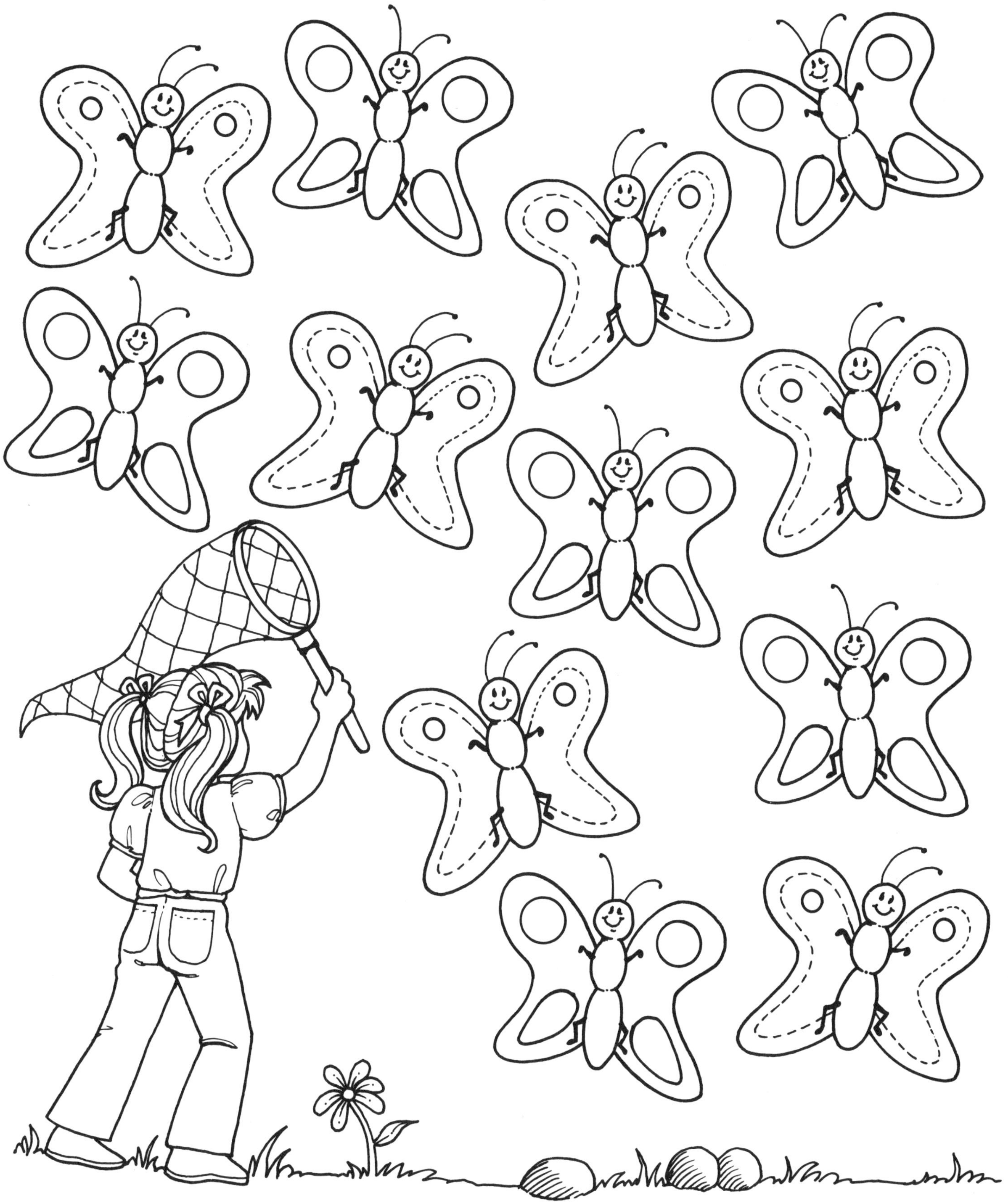

Same – Different   Name _____

✏️ the top teddy bear: 1 – **brown** 2 – **red**
3 – **blue** 4 – **green** 5 – **yellow**

✏️ this teddy bear to look the same as the top one.

Same – Different   Name _____

 and  the matching kite halves. ✏ each kite.

Same – Different   Name _____

🖍 the first row. 🖍 a line from each ice cream cone to another of the same size. 🖍 it the same colors.

Same – Different   Name _____

🖍 the first picture. 🖍 a blue circle around 10 things which are different in the second picture.

Same – Different

Name _____

✏️ the first picture. ✏️ each picture that is the same as the first one.

Same – Different

Name _____

Look at each group of three things in the picture. a purple **X** on the one that is different. the other two pictures.

Same – Different   Name _____

🖍 the missing parts to make the pictures look the same. 🖍 the pictures with the same colors.

Kdg. Critical Thinking, Self-Awareness IF8701   8   © 1992 Instructional Fair, Inc.

Same – Different

Name _____

✏️ Color each top letter and number. Use the same color to color the same letter or number in that row.

B (yellow)	4 (purple)	H (green)	8 (red)	R (blue)
B	3	E	8	P
D	4	H	8	R
B	4	H	2	J
B	5	H	7	R
C	4	T	8	R

Same – Different   Name _____

Look at the shadow shapes in the first row. ✏️ a line to match the shadow with the picture it matches.

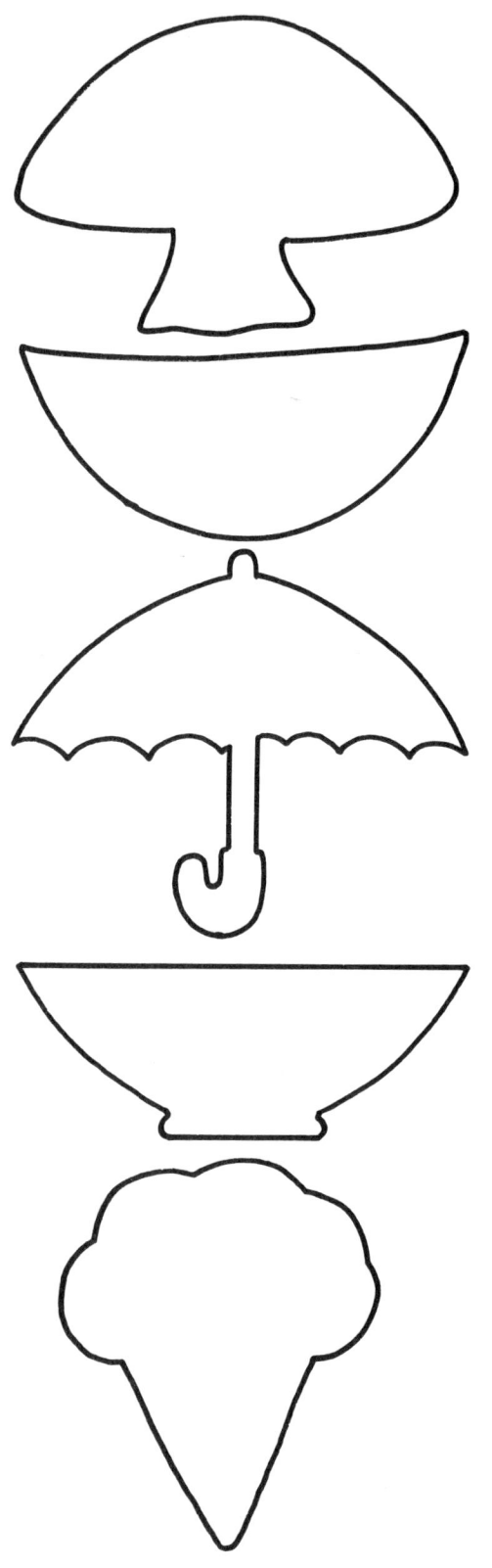

Direction: Left – Right   Name _____

🖍 red – things going to the right
       🖍 blue – things going to the left

Kdg. Critical Thinking, Self-Awareness IF8701   © 1992 Instructional Fair, Inc.

Position: Open – Closed   Name _____

✏️ and ✂️ and 🍶 each picture to show open or closed.

Position: Upside Down   Name _____

🖍 the 10 things that are upside down.

Kdg. Critical Thinking, Self-Awareness IF8701   © 1992 Instructional Fair, Inc

Position: First – Middle – Last Name _____

Look at each group of three things in the picture.
In each group: 🖍 green – **first**
🖍 purple – **middle**
🖍 orange – **last**

Position: Under – On Between – In

Name _____

and and each picture in the correct place.

Classifying: Pairs

Name _____

✏️ a line to match the things that go together.

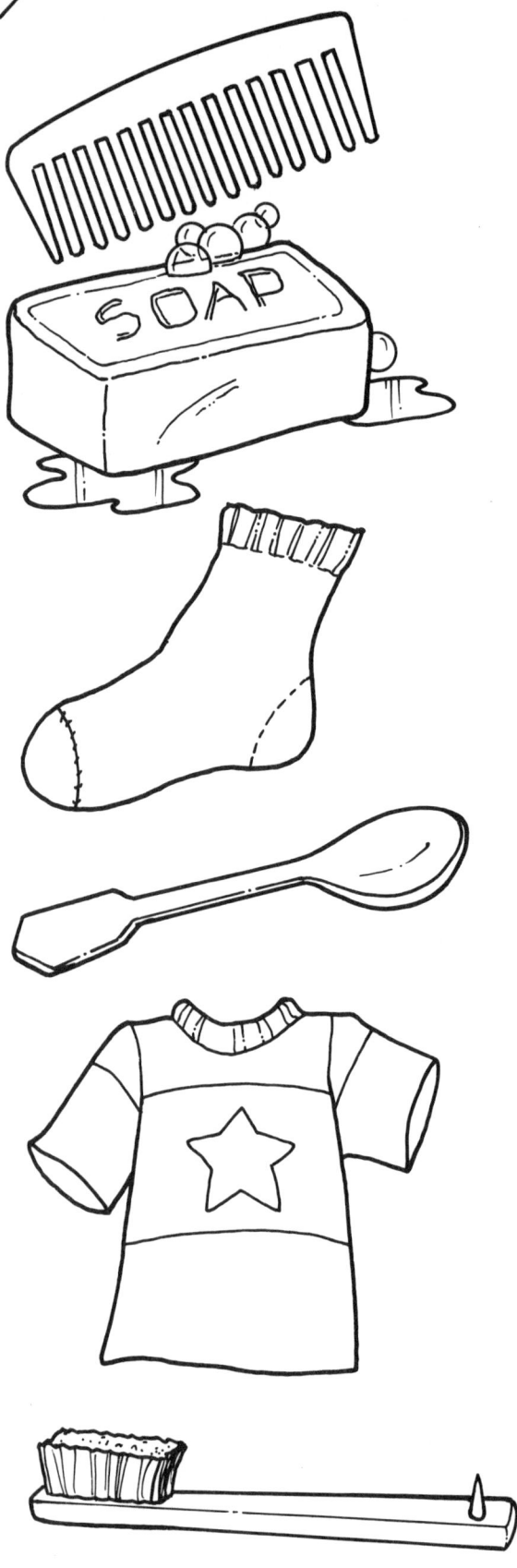

Classifying: Things by color

Name _____

🖍 each crayon. 🖍 the things that can be that color.

Classifying: Animals   Name _____

✏️ a red X on the animal that does not belong in each picture. ✏️ the animals that do belong.

Classifying: Food   Name _____

✏️ and ✂️ and 🍶 the food you might take on a picnic.

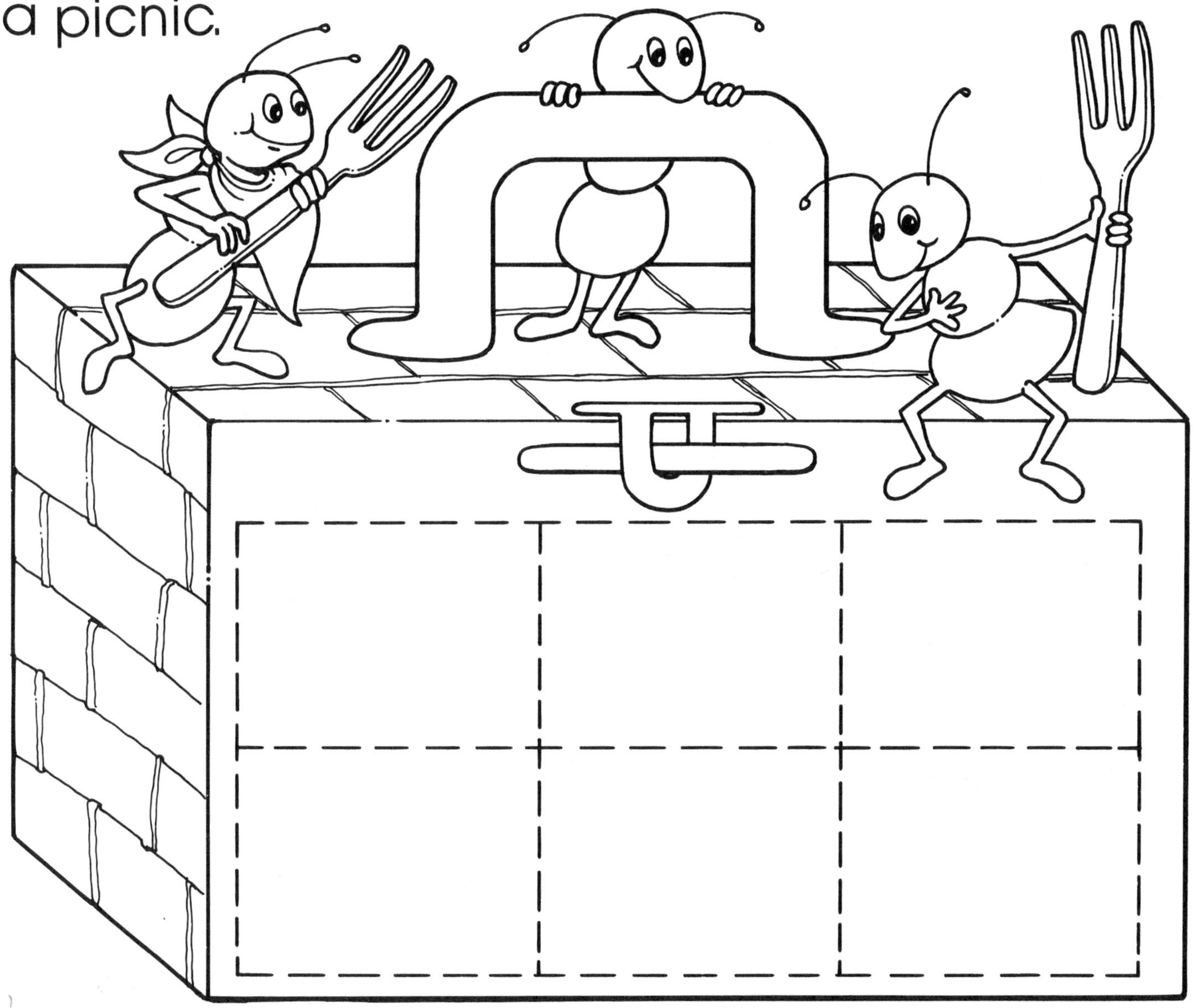

Classifying: Music

Name _____

✏️ a line from the 🎵 to each thing that makes music.

Classifying: Light

Name _____

✏️ a circle around 10 things that give light.

Classifying: Senses　　　　Name _____

✏ and ✂ and 🍶 each picture to tell which sense is used.

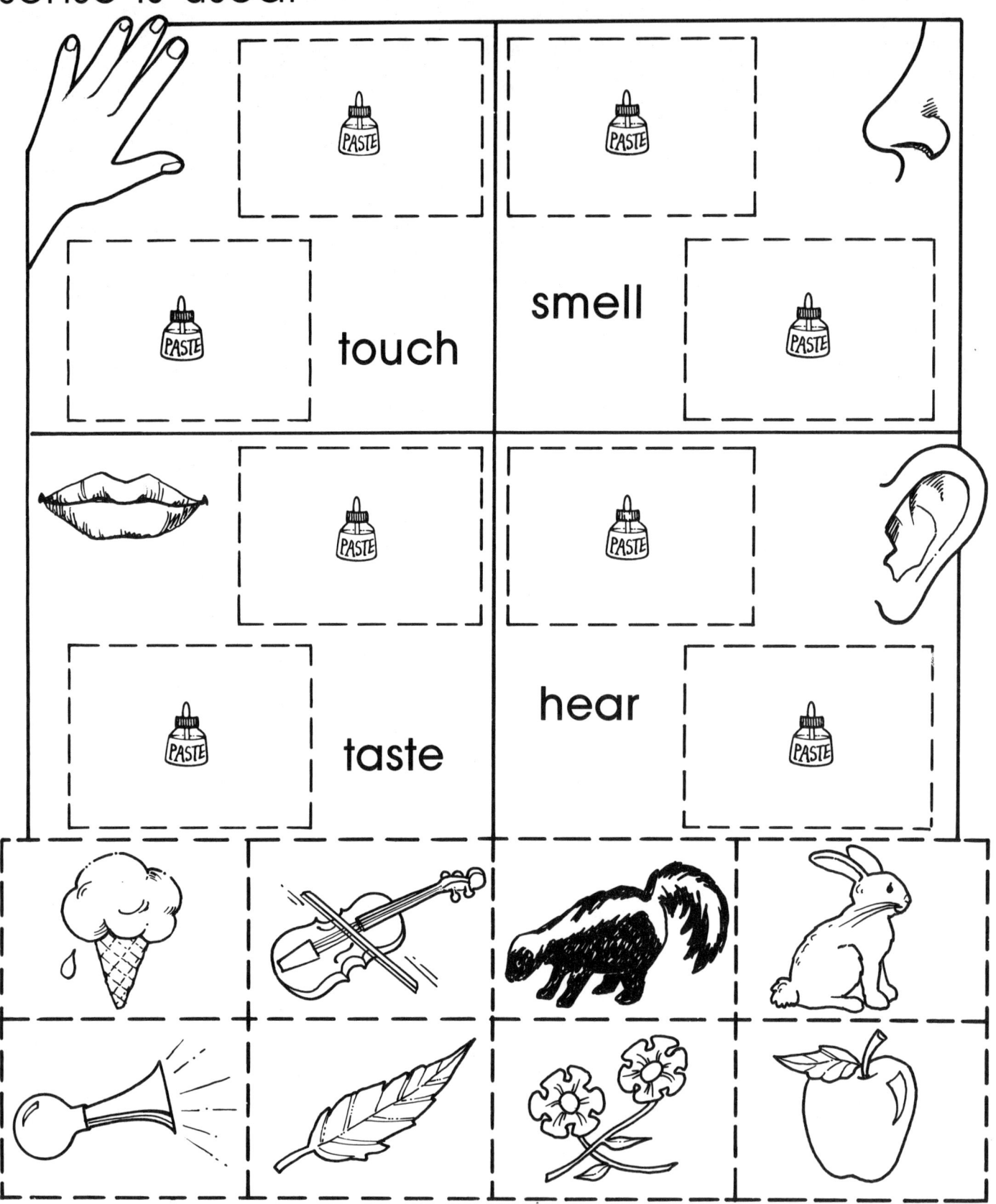

Classifying: Food

Name _____

🖍 the bear red. 🖍 a red circle around each sweet food to find the path to the lollipop house. 🖍 the bunny yellow. 🖍 a yellow circle around each vegetable to find the path to the garden.

Classifying: Does not belong Name _____

Look at each scene. ✏️ a green **X** on each thing that does not belong.

Kdg. Critical Thinking, Self-Awareness IF8701

Sequencing

Name _____

🖍 1-2-3 to put the pictures in order.
🖍 the pictures.

SEQUENCING

Name _____

 and  and the pictures in 1-2-3 order.

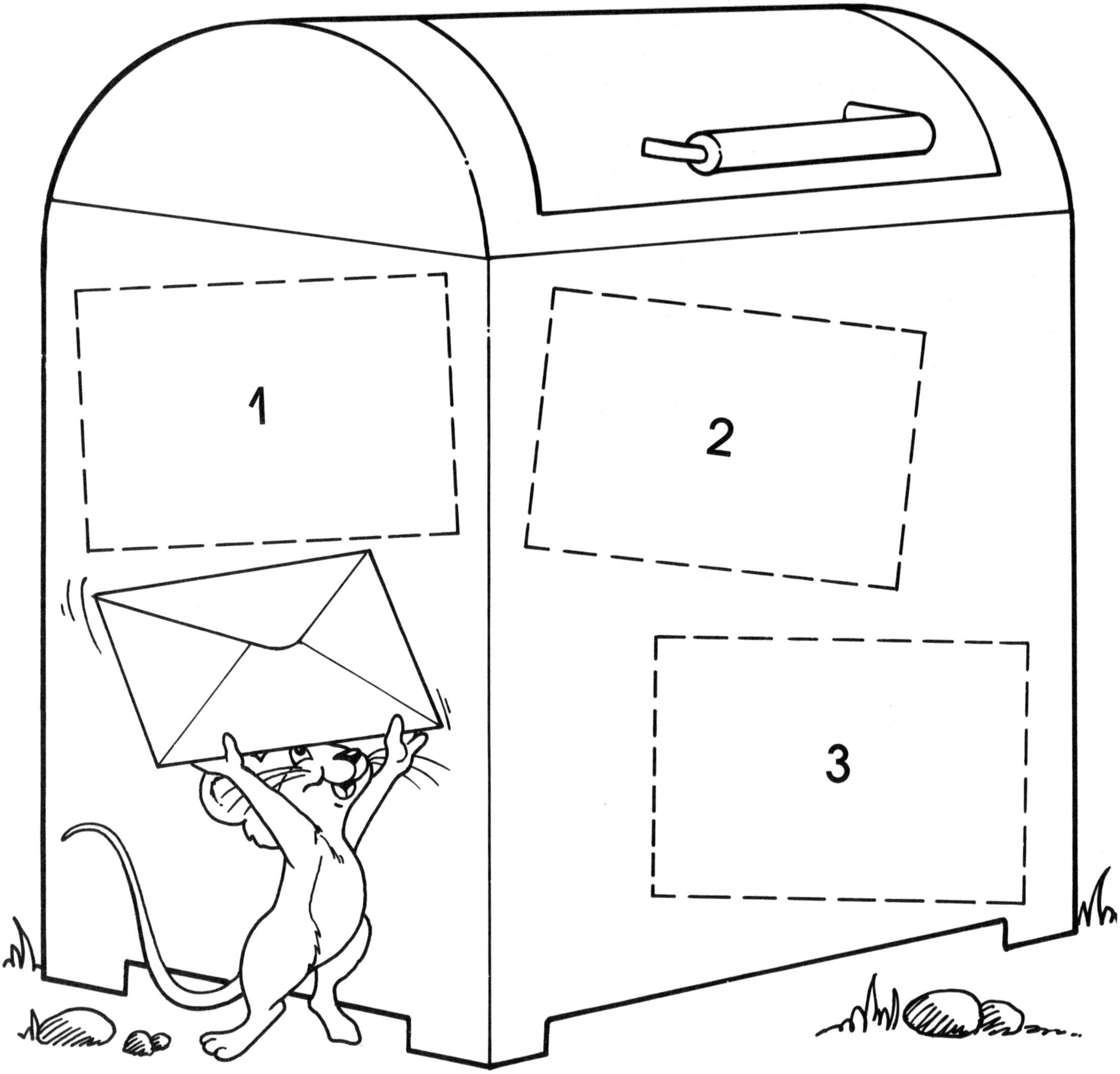

SEQUENCING

Name _____

✏️ the numbers and pictures. 🖍️ a line from each number to a picture to put the pictures in 1-2-3-4 order.

Kdg. Critical Thinking, Self-Awareness IF8701   27   © 1992 Instructional Fair, Inc.

Sequencing

🖍 and ✂ and 🍶 each 🪁 by the correct number.

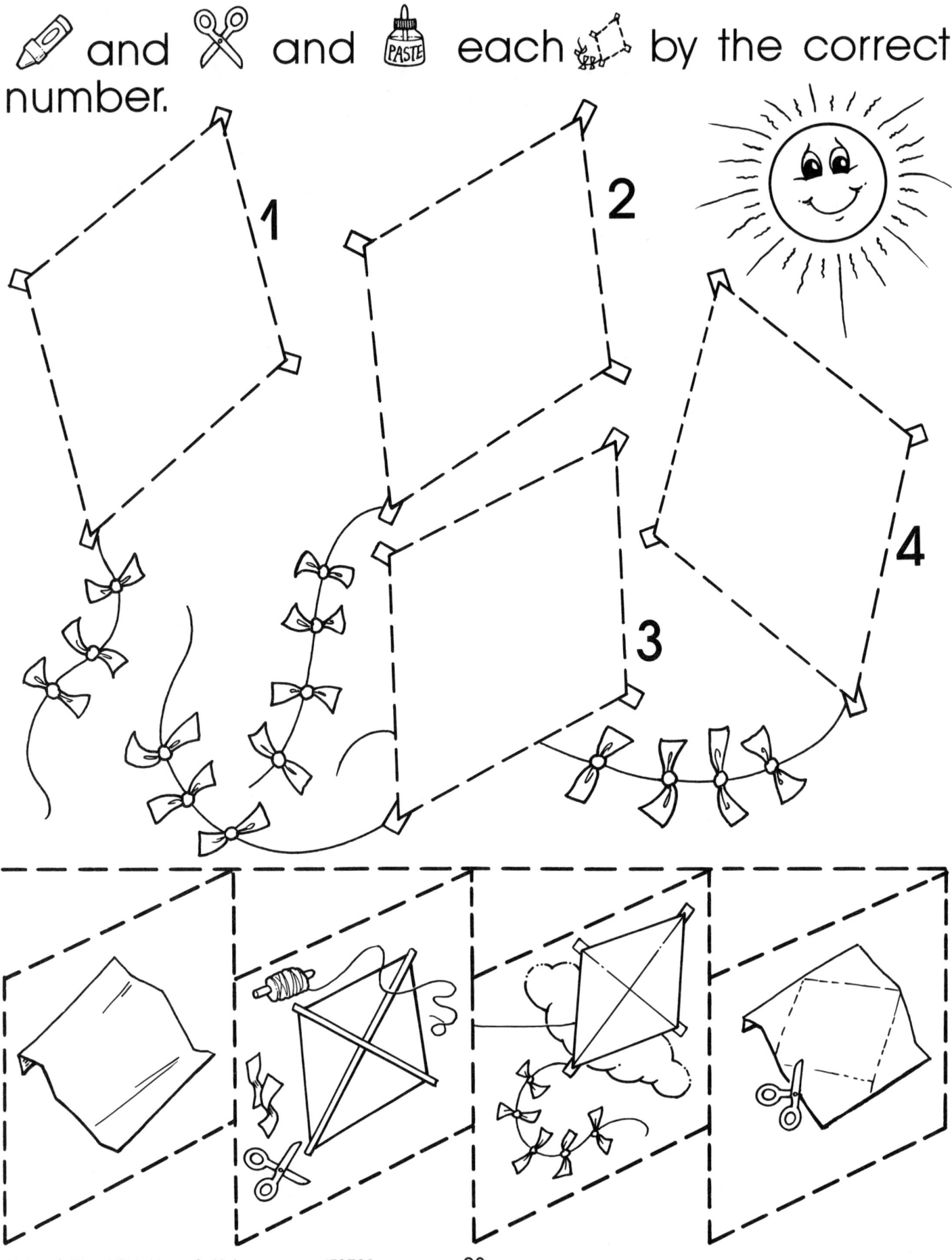

SEQUENCING

Name _____

✏️ and ✂️ and 🍯 the right picture to show 1-2-3 order.

Sequencing   Name _____

🖍 1-2-3-4 in the O's to put the pictures in order.
🖍 the pictures: **1 - red   2 - yellow   3 - green   4 - blue.**

SEQUENCING

Name _____

✏️ and ✂️ and 🫙 the pictures in 1-2-3-4 order.

Sequencing   Name _____

✂ and 🍶PASTE the numbers to put the pictures in 1-2-3-4 order.

Sequencing   Name _____

✂ and 🫙PASTE the pictures in 1-2-3-4 order. ✏ the pictures.

1	2
🫙PASTE	🫙PASTE
3	4
🫙PASTE	🫙PASTE

Kdg. Critical Thinking, Self-Awareness IF8701 © 1992 Instructional Fair, Inc.

Following Directions   Name _____

 the spaces: 1 - brown   2 - yellow   3 - green
                     4 - orange   5 - purple

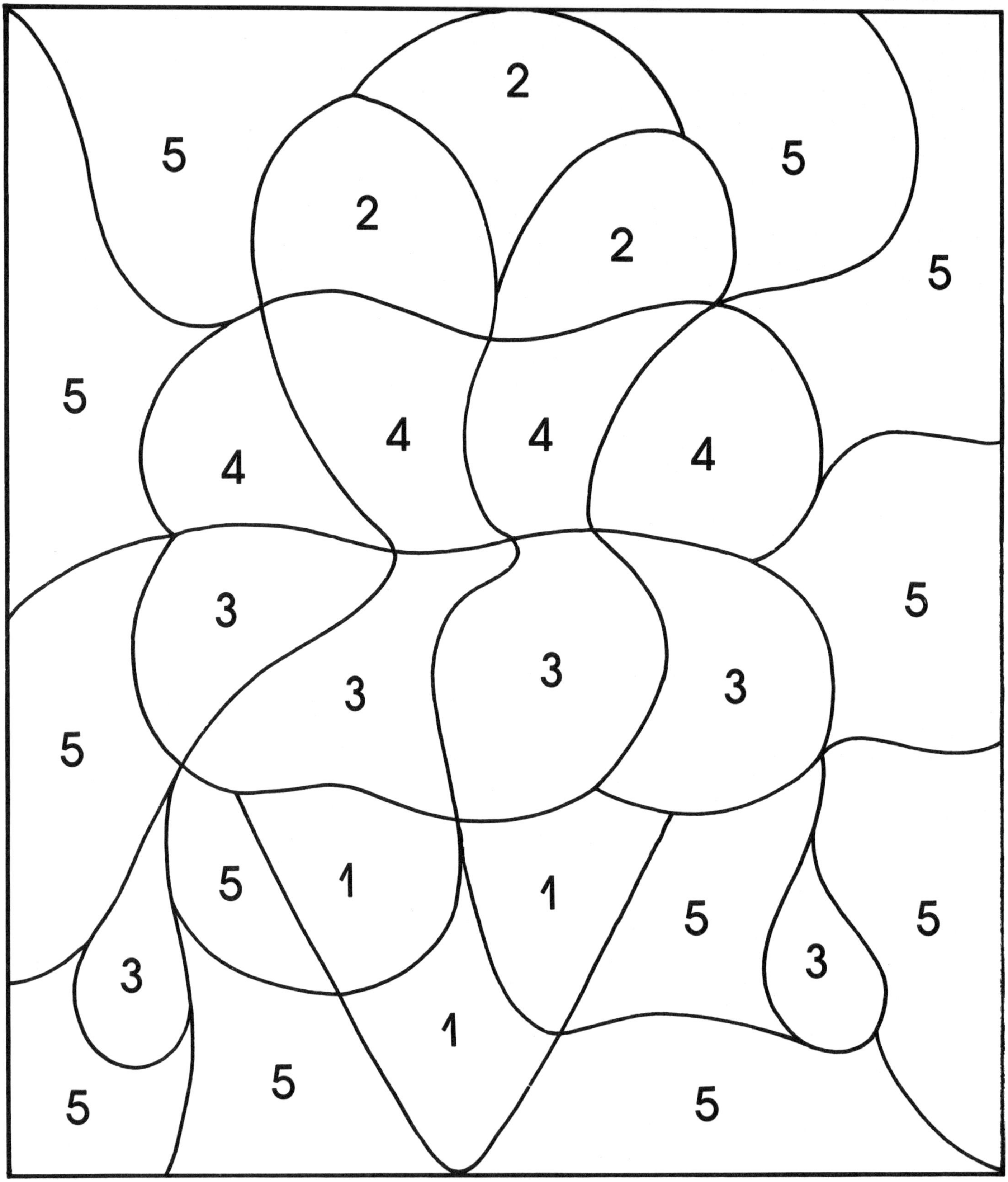

Following Directions   Name _____

Find the 10 "hidden" mice. ✏ the mice:
1 - red   2 - brown   3 - green   4 - orange

Following Directions

Name _____

✏️ and ✂️ and 🫙 the O's.
🖍️ and 🖍️ the ⌒'s.

- green
- red
- orange (PASTE)
- blue
- blue
- yellow (PASTE)
- orange
- purple
- red
- green
- yellow
- green
- red (PASTE)
- blue
- purple

- red
- orange
- yellow

Following Directions Name _____

✏️ a line to follow the alphabet from A to Z in the correct order.

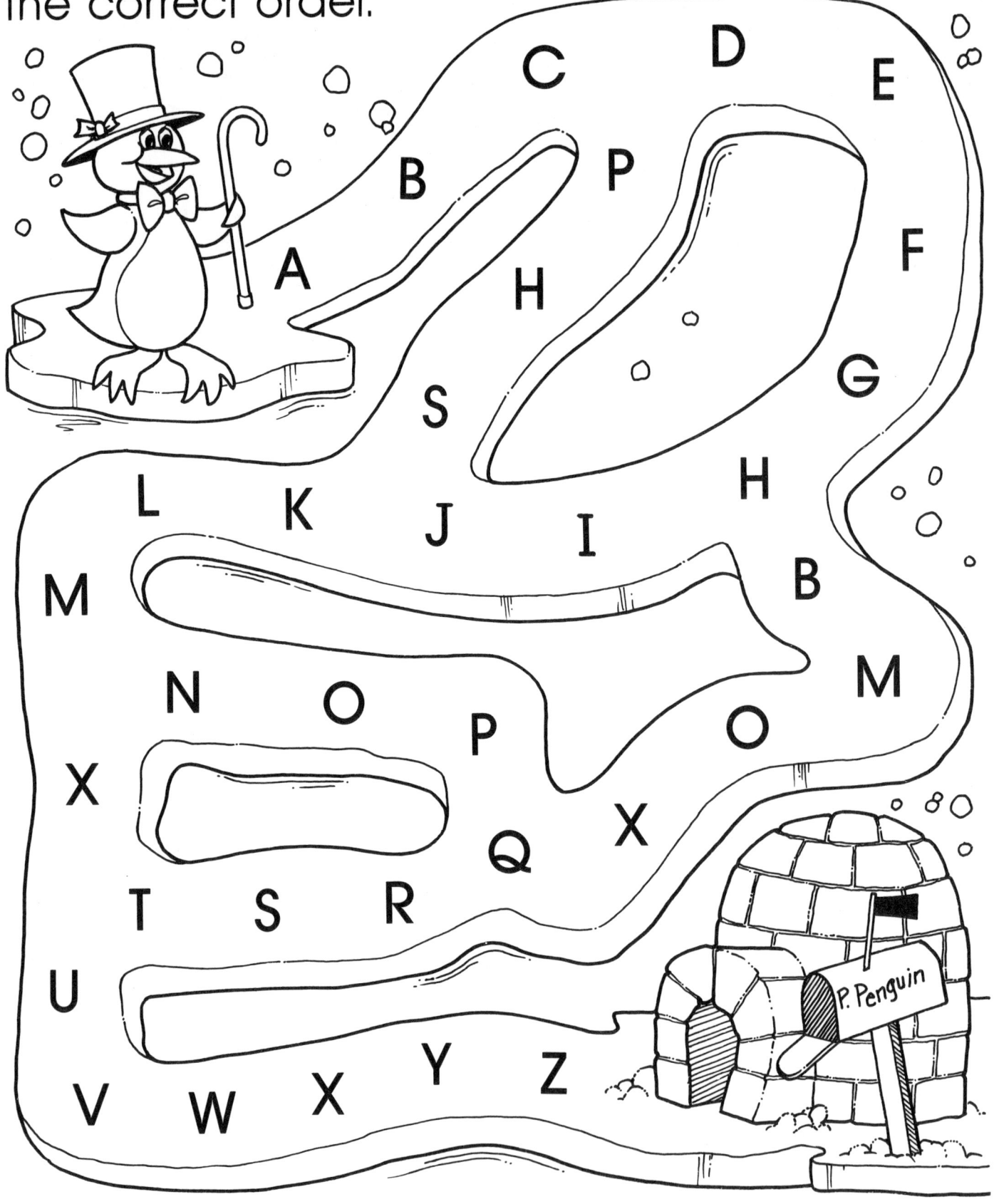

Following Directions   Name _____

 the dot on each butterfly.  the other dots.
✂ and 🧴 the matching dot on each butterfly.

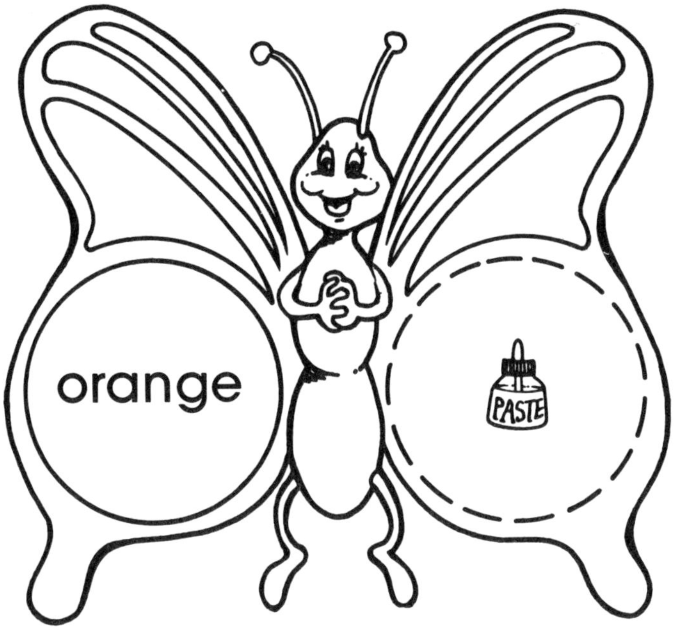

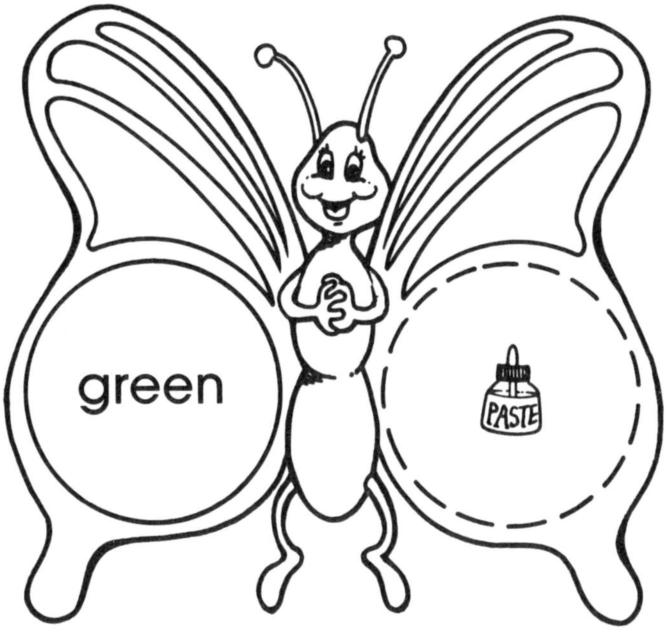

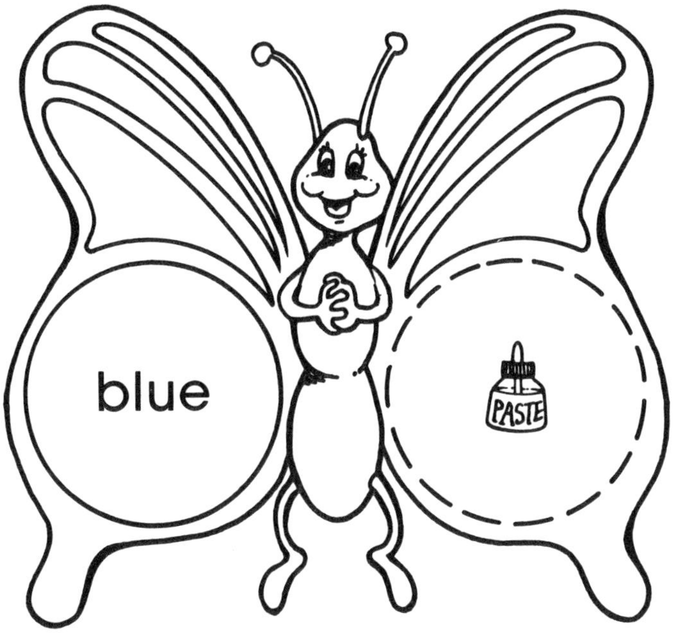

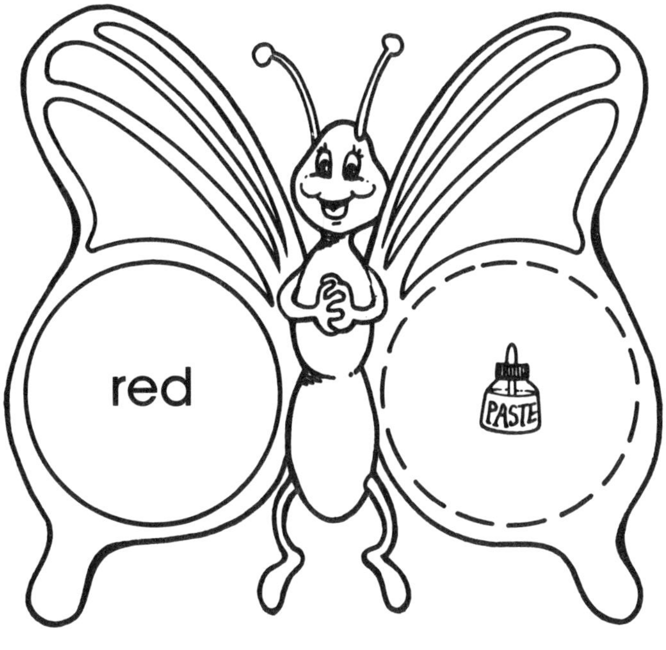

orange   green

blue   red

green   orange   blue   red

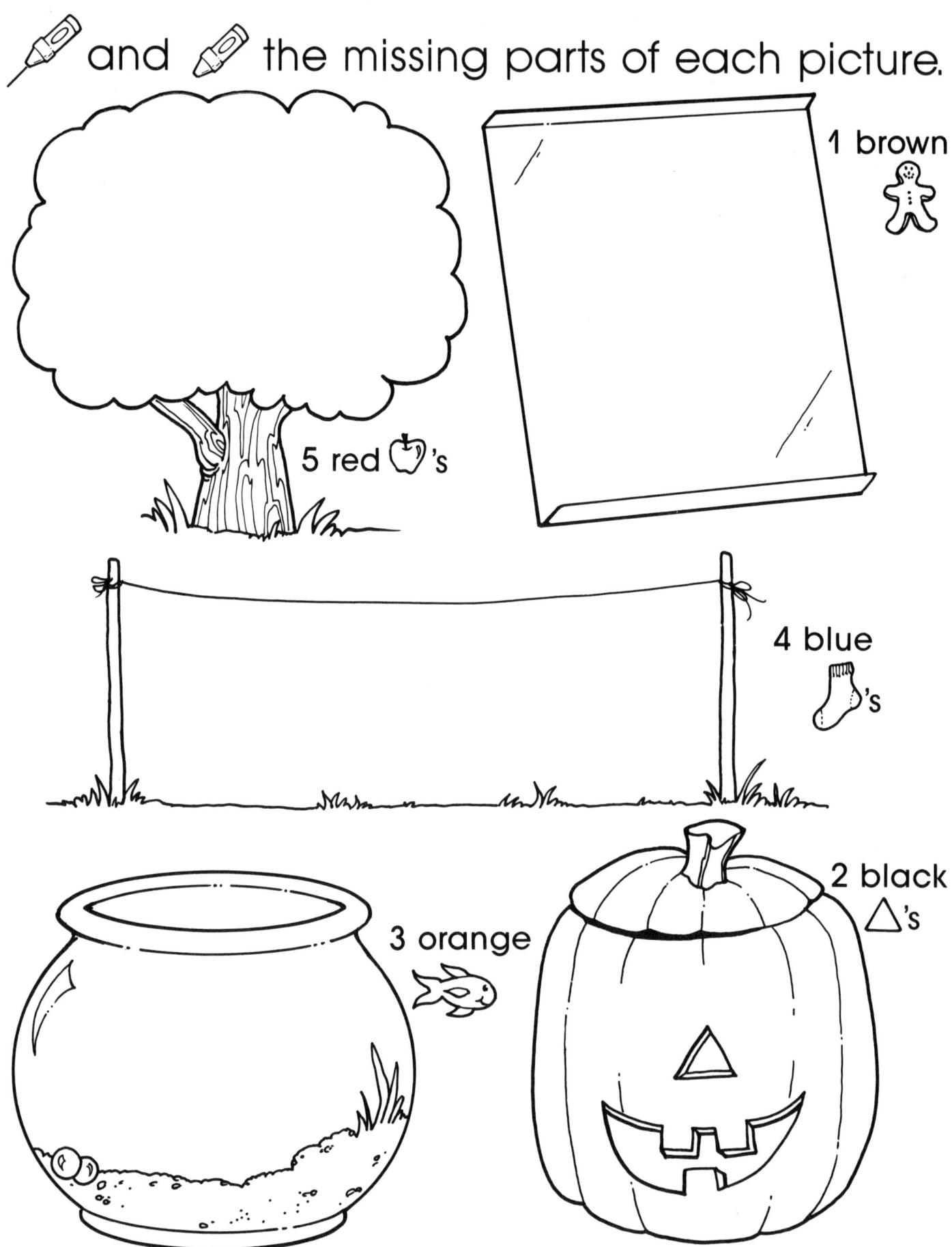

Following Directions   Name _____

✏️ the right pictures in each row. Use the right color.

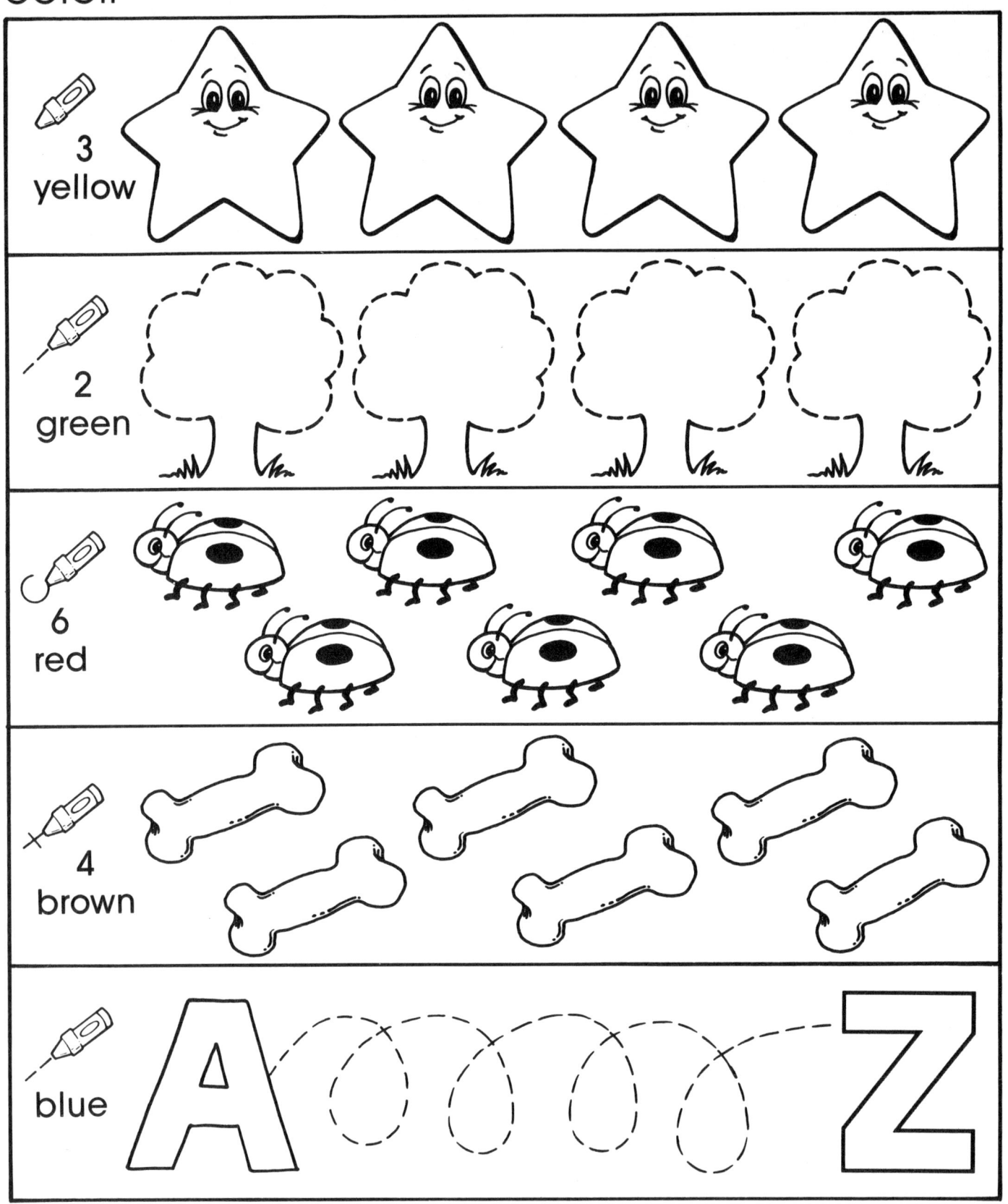

3 yellow

2 green

6 red

4 brown

blue

Following Directions

Name _____

✏️ a line to connect the dots from **A - Z**.
Use the right color for each part of the line.

A - E red **F - J** yellow **K - O** blue **P - T** green **U - Z** purple

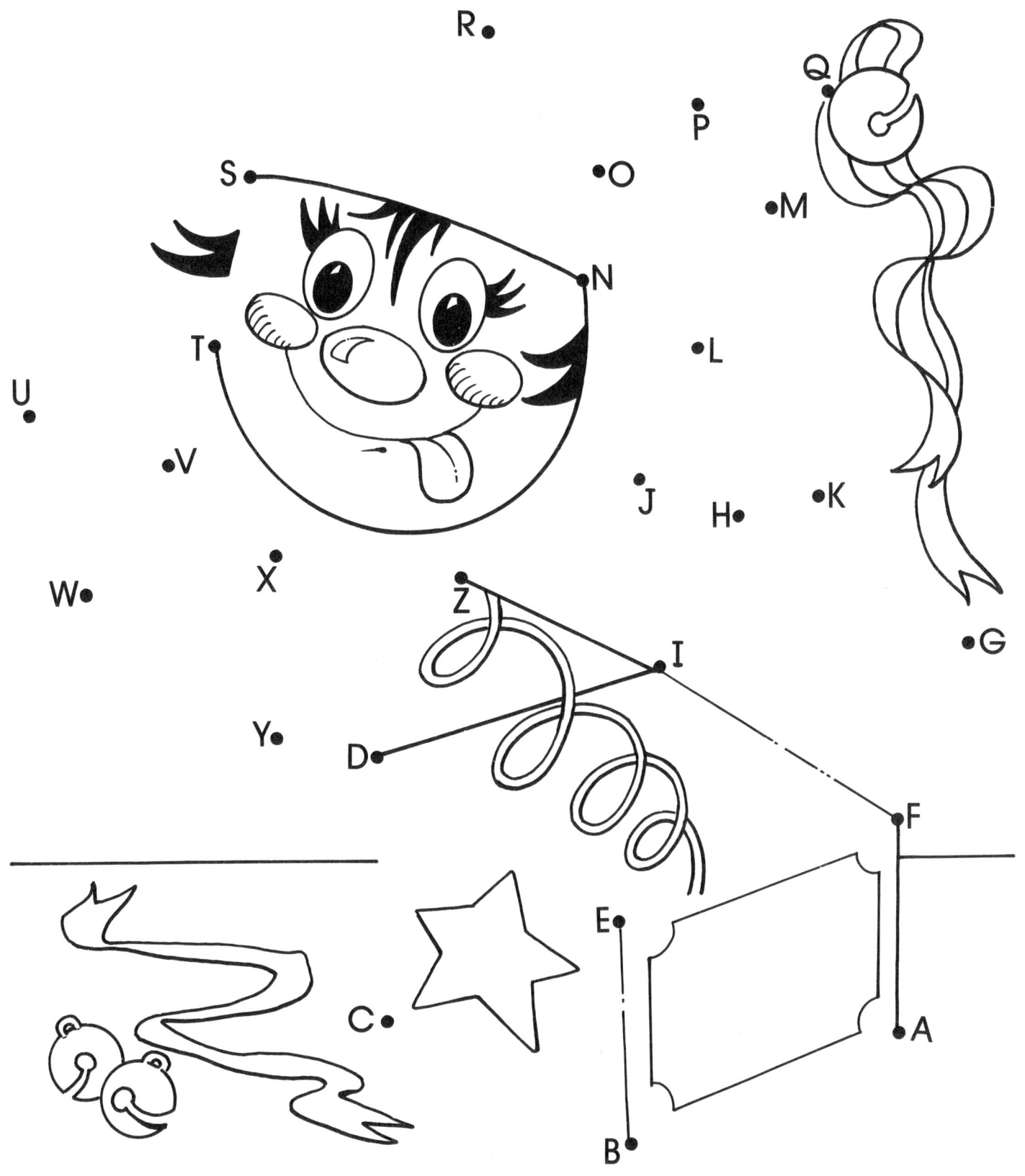

Kdg. Critical Thinking, Self-Awareness IF8701 © 1992 Instructional Fair, Inc.

Opposites Name _____

✏️ a line to match the opposite pictures. 🖍️ the pictures to match.

Kdg. Critical Thinking, Self-Awareness IF8701

Opposites

Name _____

🖍 and ✂ and 🍯 each picture to show opposites.

Predicting Outcome   Name _____

Look at the pictures in the first row. ✏️ a line to the picture that shows what will happen.

Kdg. Critical Thinking, Self-Awareness IF8701   © 1992 Instructional Fair, Inc.

Predicting Outcome

Name _____

🖍 the 1, 2, 3 pictures. 🖍 and 🖍 the last picture to show what will happen.

Predicting Outcome

Name _____

✏️ the first pictures. ✏️ and ✂️ and 🗲 the pictures to show what will happen.

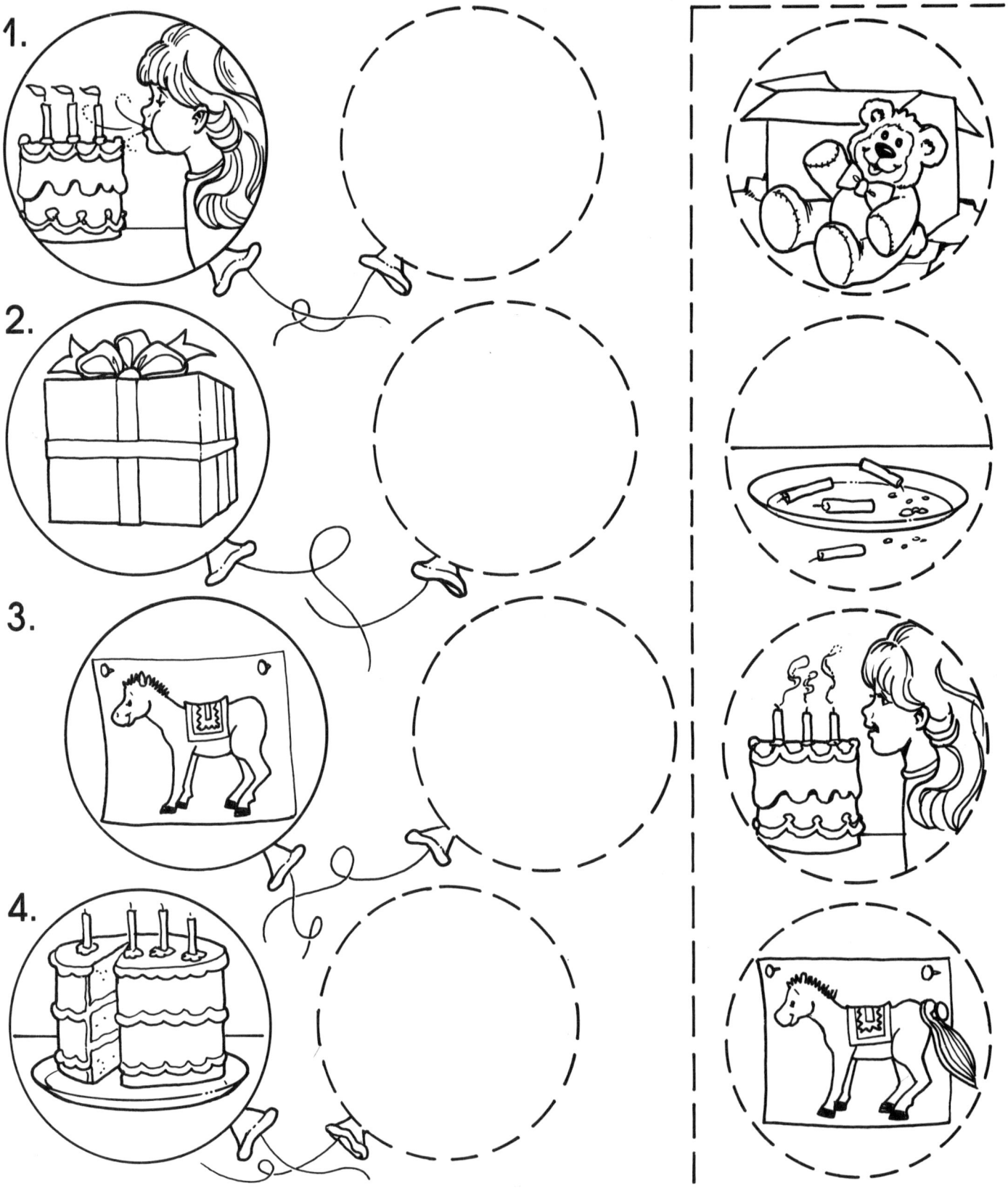

Predicting Outcome

Name _____

🖍 each picture. 🖍 a picture to show what will happen.

Drawing Conclusions

Name _____

✏ each picture. ✂ and 🧴 a face in each ◯ to tell how the person feels.

Drawing Conclusions

Name _____

✏️ the first picture. ✂️ and ✏️ the picture ending that goes best with the first picture.

Finding Incorrect Concepts

Name _____

Look at the picture. 🖍 a red circle around 10 things which are **not** right.

Kdg. Critical Thinking, Self-Awareness IF8701 © 1992 Instructional Fair, Inc.

Finding Incorrect Concepts

Help the mother bear find her 5 little bears in the park. ✏️ a red X on the little bears which do not look right. ✏️ the other 5 little bears and ✏️ a line from each to the mother bear.

Real and Fantasy   Name _____

Look at the picture. ✏️ a purple circle around the 10 things which are make-believe and not real.

Kdg. Critical Thinking, Self-Awareness IF8701   54   © 1992 Instructional Fair, Inc.

Self   Name _____

🖍 and 🖍 a picture of how you look.

🖍 your name.

Self

✂ and 🫙 the birthday cake that tells how old you are.

🖍 your age on the balloon.

🖍 and 🖍 a gift in the box that you would like to have.

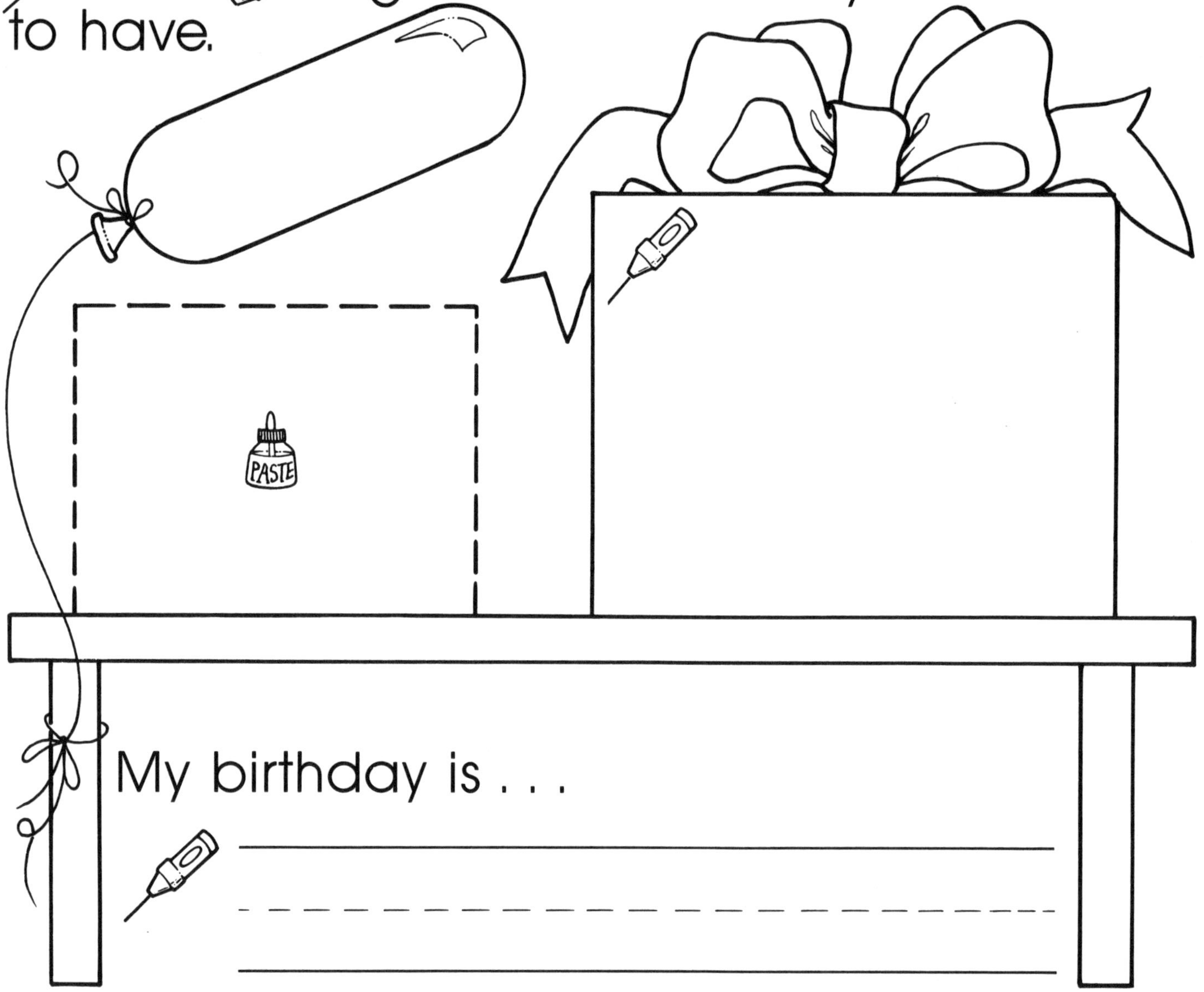

My birthday is . . .

Self

Name _____

✏️ and 🖍️ a picture of where you live.

My Home

🖍️ your address.

Self   Name _____

✏️ and 🖍 a picture of each of your favorites.

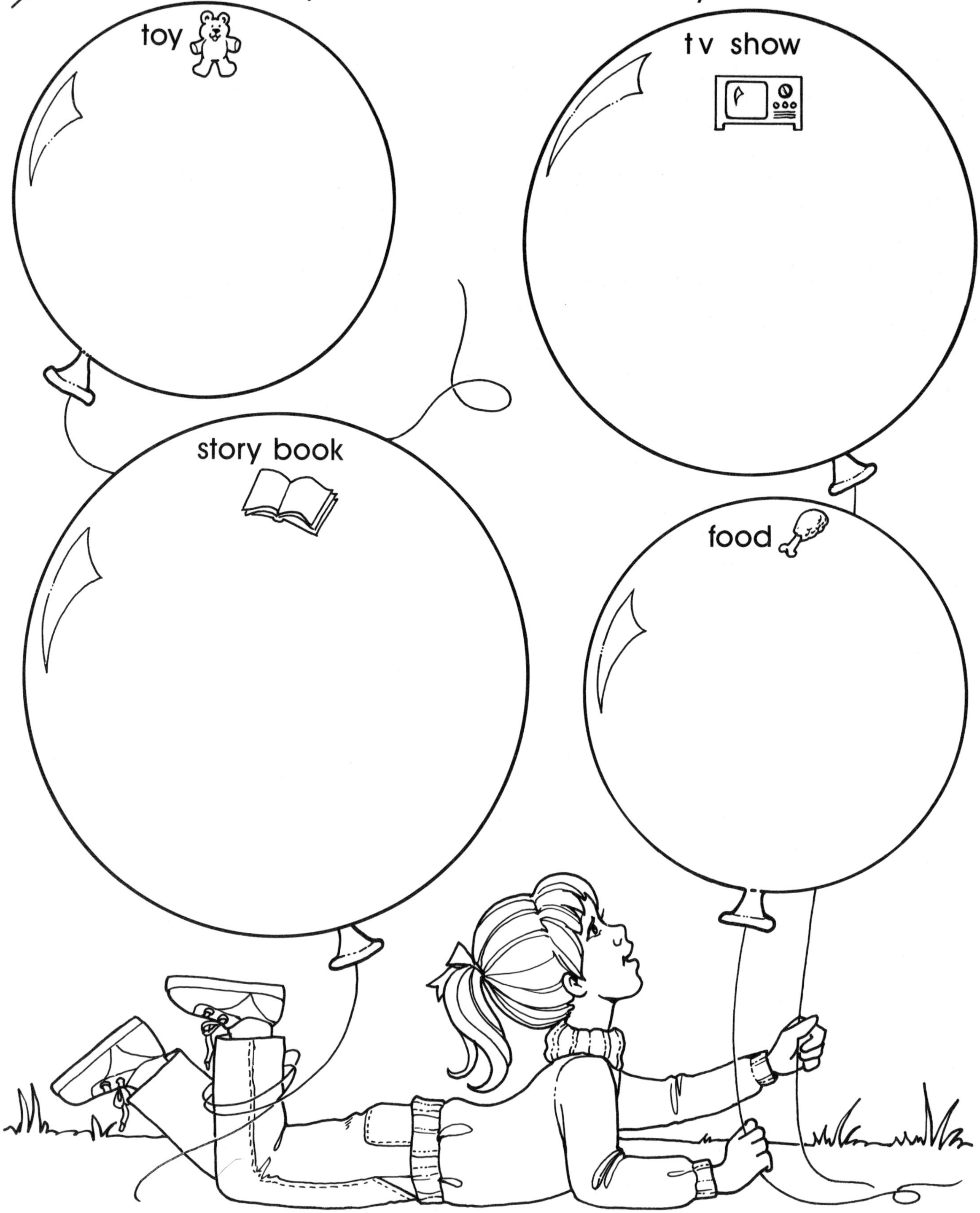

toy

tv show

story book

food

Self   Name _____

✏️ your telephone number.

_____

- -

_____

Count the telephones in each picture. ✏️ the number in the ☐ . 🖍️ the telephones.

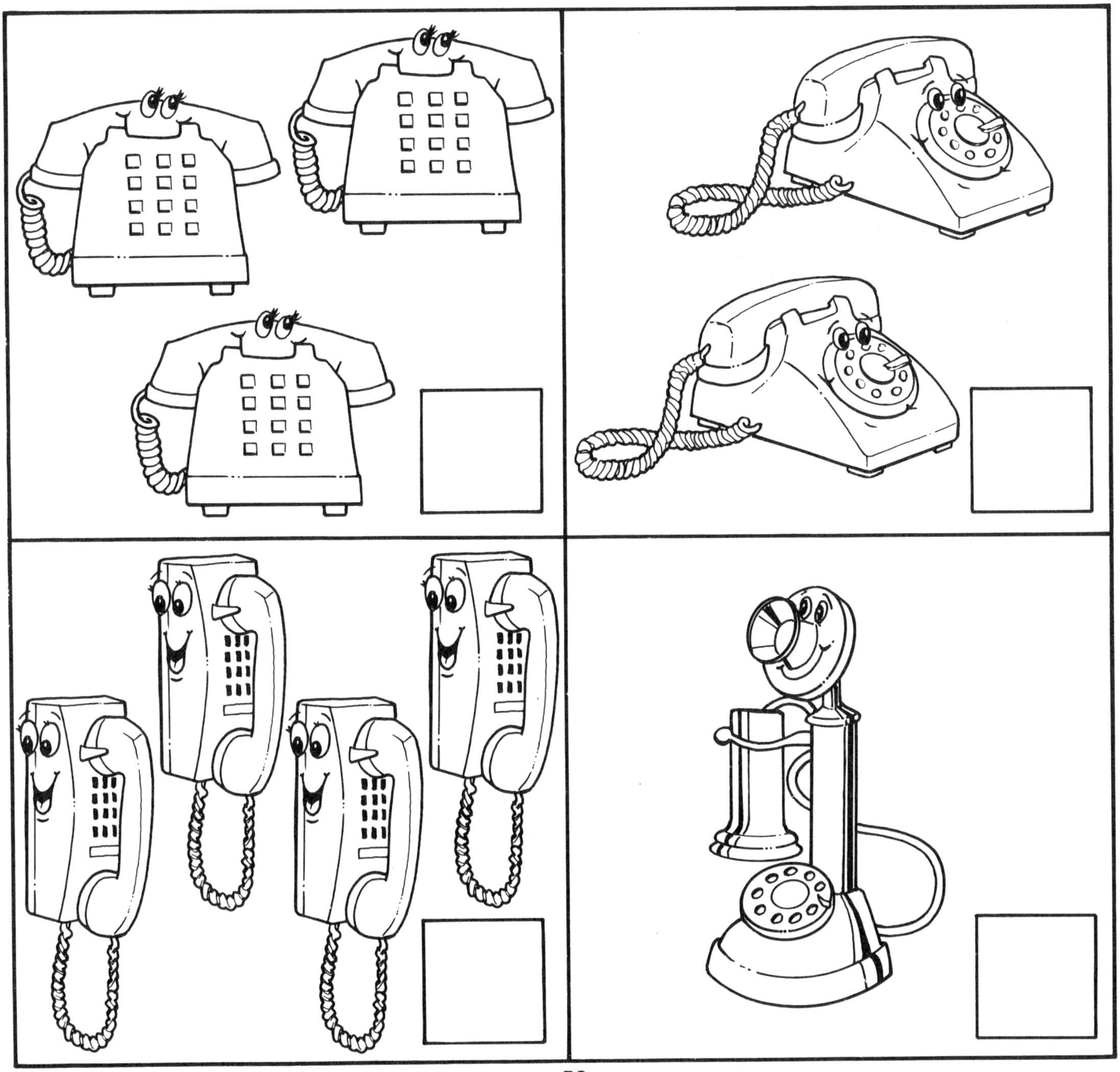

Self   Name _____

✂ and 🫙PASTE the things you would use for each activity.
🖍 the two activities that you like the best.

Self

Name _____

Everyone is special. Everyone is a star. ✏ the ☆ around each child. 🖍 the pictures to see how each child is special.

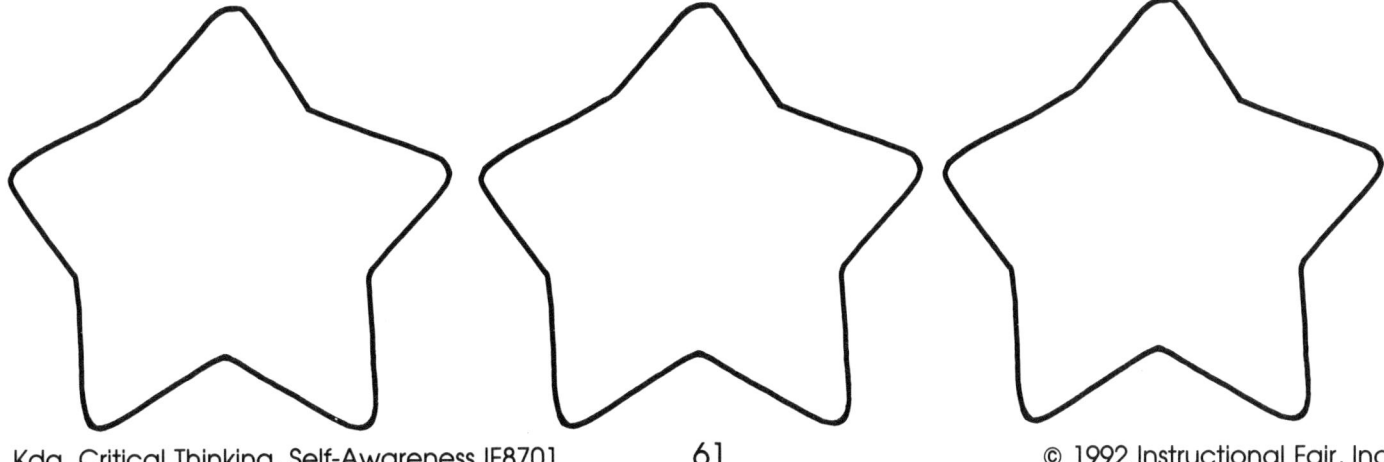

🖍 and 🖍 three pictures to show how you are special.

Family						Name _____

 and a picture of your family.

┌───┐
│   │
│   │
│   │
│   │
│   │
│   │
│   │
└───┘

 the pictures that show what your family likes to do.

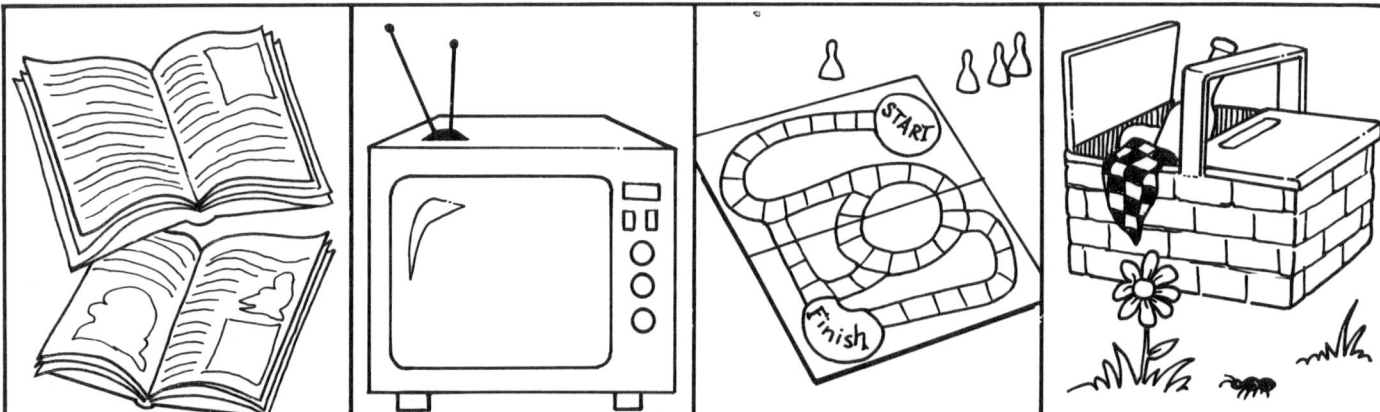

Family   Name _____

✏️ the first name of each person.

_____   _____
Grandfather   Grandfather

_____   _____
Grandmother   Grandmother

_____   _____
Mom   Dad

_____
Me

Ask your family to help you!

My Family Tree

Family   Name _____

Grandparents are fun to visit. ✏️ a line from A–Z to show the way to the grandparents' house.

Kdg. Critical Thinking, Self-Awareness IF8701 © 1992 Instructional Fair, Inc.

Family

Name _____

✏️ the ♥'s red. ✂️ and 🧴 a ♥ on each picture that shows how your family loves and cares for each other.

Family   Name _____

Look at the ways you can help at home. ✏ a line to match each picture with the things you would need to help.

Growing Up

Name _____

✏️ and ✂️ and 🍶 the people in a row from large to small.

Growing Up

Name _____

✂ and 🍯 the numbers to put the pictures in 1, 2, 3, 4 order.

Growing Up

Name _____

✏️ and ✂️ and 🏷️PASTE the pictures that show ways you can help others.

BIG HELPER AWARDS

Growing Up

Name _____

✏️ and ✂️ and 🍶 each thing that you might pack to sleep overnight at a friend's house.

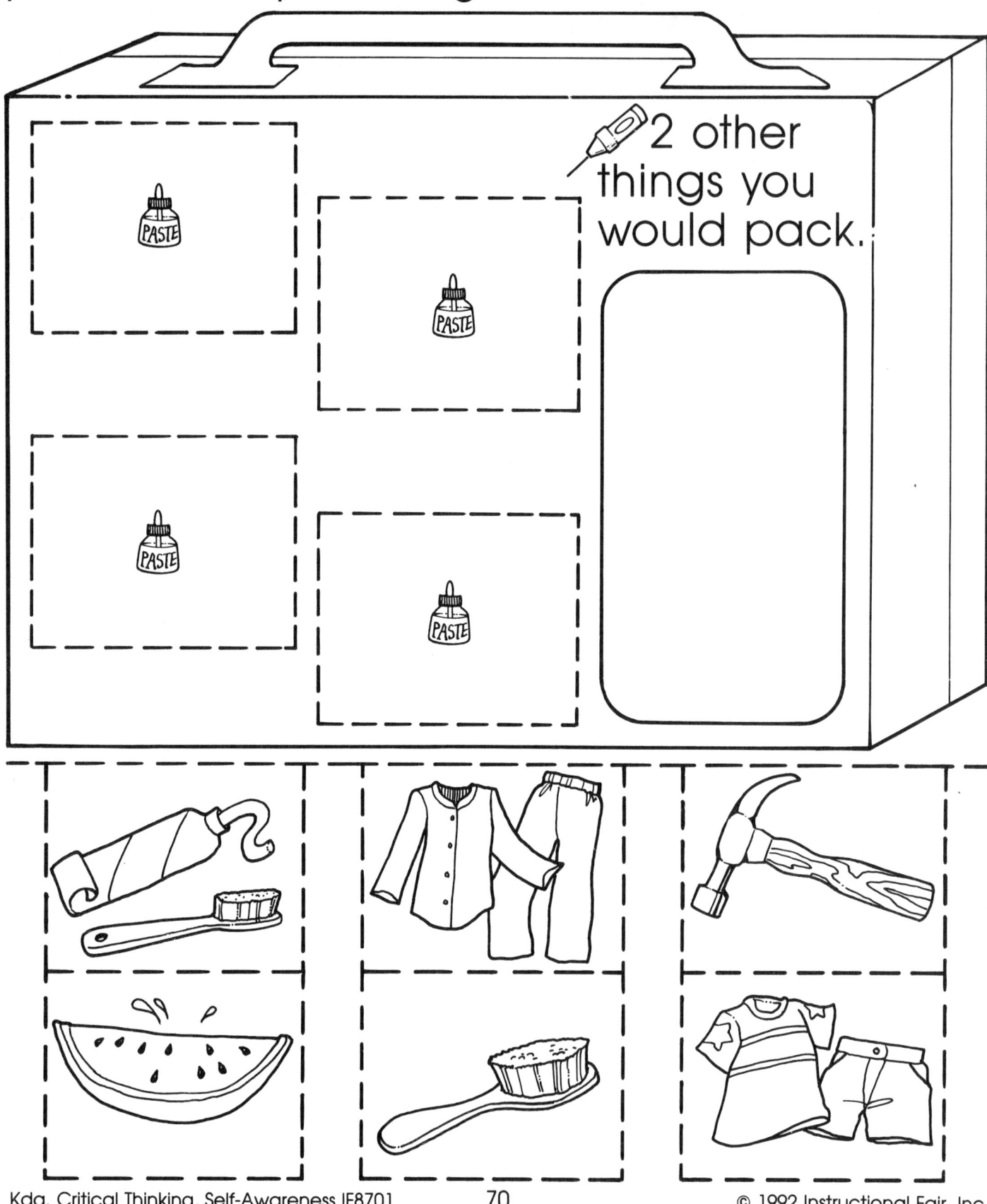

Growing Up

Name _____

🖍 the money in each picture.

LEMONADE 5¢

Count the ¢'s in the bank.

🖍 10 ¢'s in the bank.

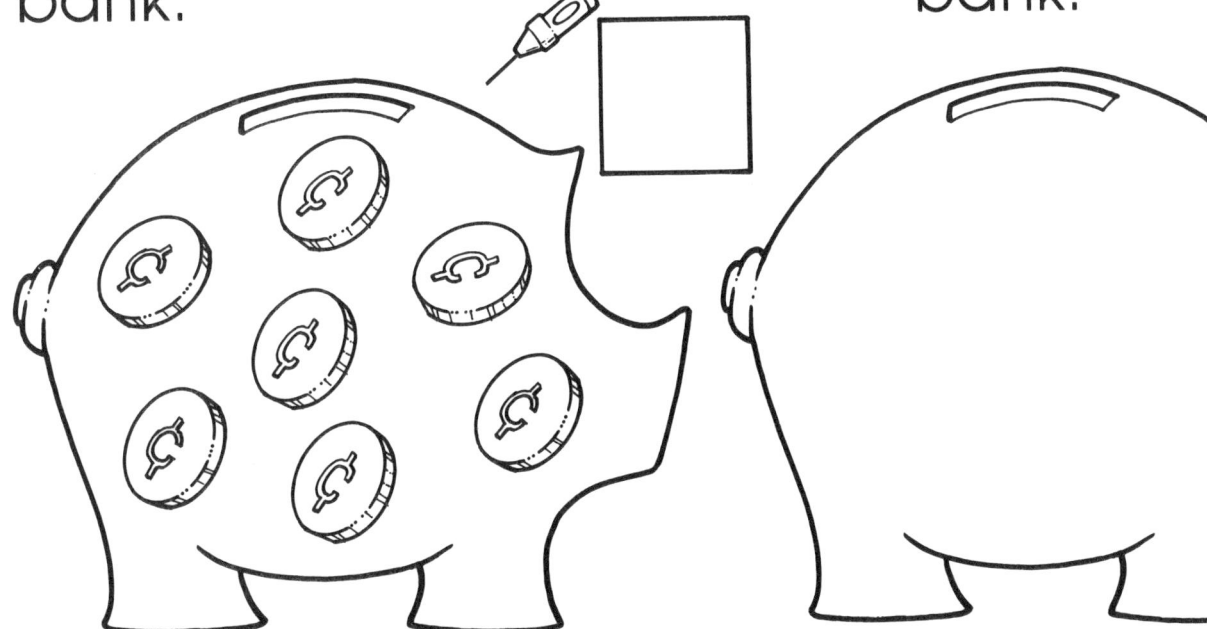

Growing Up

Name _____

🖍 each picture of a pet. 🖍 your favorite pet.
🖍 an **x** on the animals which would not be good pets.

🖍 the pictures that show the way to care for a pet.

Growing Up

Name _____

🖍 each thing in the bedroom that needs to be cleaned up.

🖍 the picture of the clean bedroom.

Kdg. Critical Thinking, Self-Awareness IF8701

Growing Up

Name _____

✏ the picture that shows what each child should do.

Growing Up

Name _____

It is fun to help shop for groceries. ✏️ an **x** on each thing which does not belong in the grocery store.

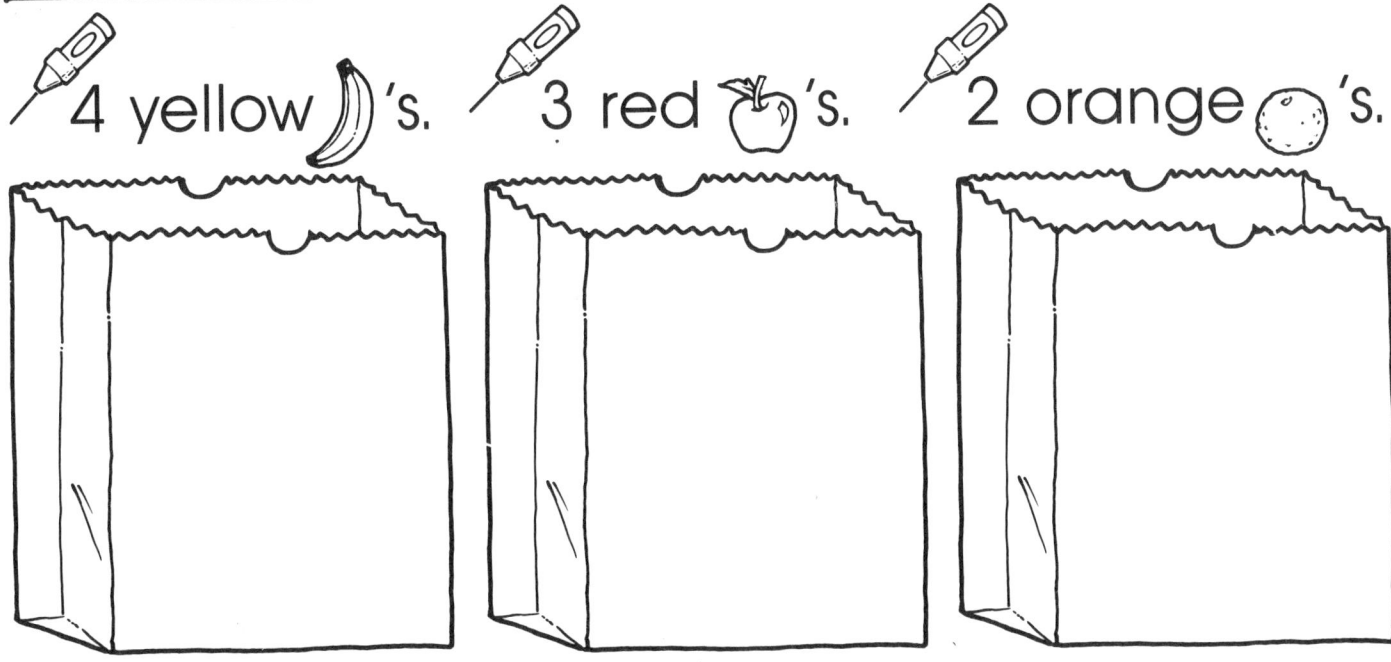

✏️ 4 yellow 🍌's.   ✏️ 3 red 🍎's.   ✏️ 2 orange 🍊's.

Growing Up   Name _____

✏ and ✏ a picture that shows teddy bear what you want to be when you grow up.

School　　　　　　　　　　　　Name _____

✏️ 1-2-3-4 in each ◯ to put the dream in order.

School   Name _____

🖍 a circle around the teacher in each picture.
🖍 your three favorite pictures to show how your teacher cares.

School   Name _____

✏️ an **x** on each thing that does not belong on the playground.

✏️ yourself enjoying your favorite activity.

School   Name _____

Which pictures show things you can do at school? ✏ each 🍎 red if it has a school picture.

✏ the pictures of your favorite school activities.

School

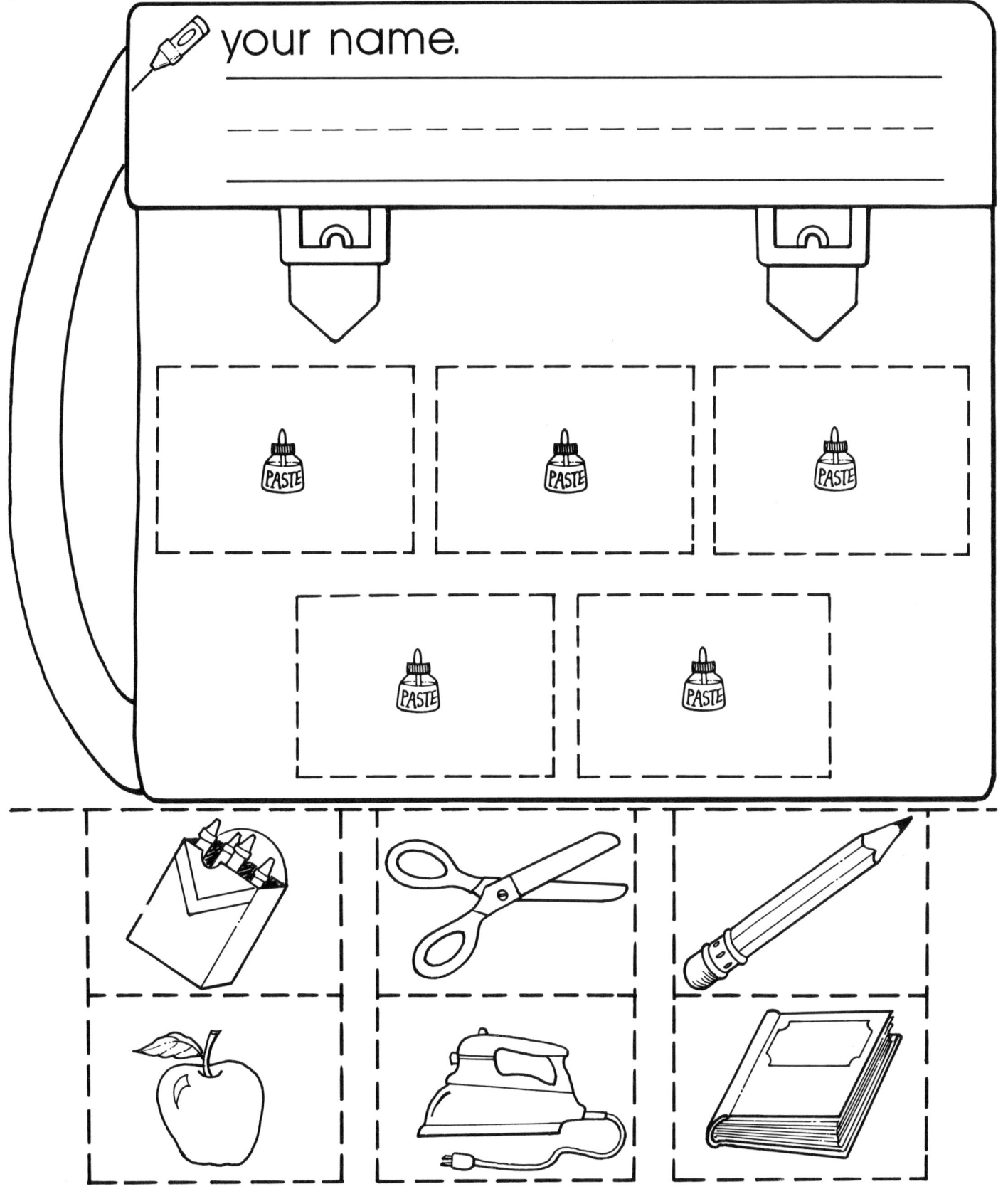

School   Name _____

 and  and : ☺ – being good
                                              ☹ – not being good. 

✏️ yellow.

Feelings

Name _____

🖍 a circle around each happy face in the crowd.

🖍 and 🖍 a happy face on the clown.

Kdg. Critical Thinking, Self-Awareness IF8701 © 1992 Instructional Fair, Inc.

Feelings

Name _____

Look at each sad person. Draw a line to each picture to show what makes each person happy.

Kdg. Critical Thinking, Self-Awareness IF8701 © 1992 Instructional Fair, Inc.

Feelings   Name _____

Sharing feels good. Count the things that are being shared. ✏ the number in the ☐.
✏ the pictures.

Feelings

✏️ a line to match the pictures to show why each child feels proud. 🖍️ the pictures.

Feelings

Name _____

✏️ and 🖍️ the picture that shows how to be honest.

Kdg. Critical Thinking, Self-Awareness IF8701 © 1992 Instructional Fair, Inc.

Feelings

Name _____

✏️ a line from the baby to each picture that shows how you can be a big helper. ✏️ the pictures.

Feelings

✏️ the pictures that show times you might be jealous.

Feelings

Name _____

*each picture of something that might scare you. and and each picture to show what could make you feel safer.

Feelings

✏️ each picture that shows why someone might feel embarrassed.

Health   Name _____

✏ and ✂ and 📋 the healthy foods on the plate.

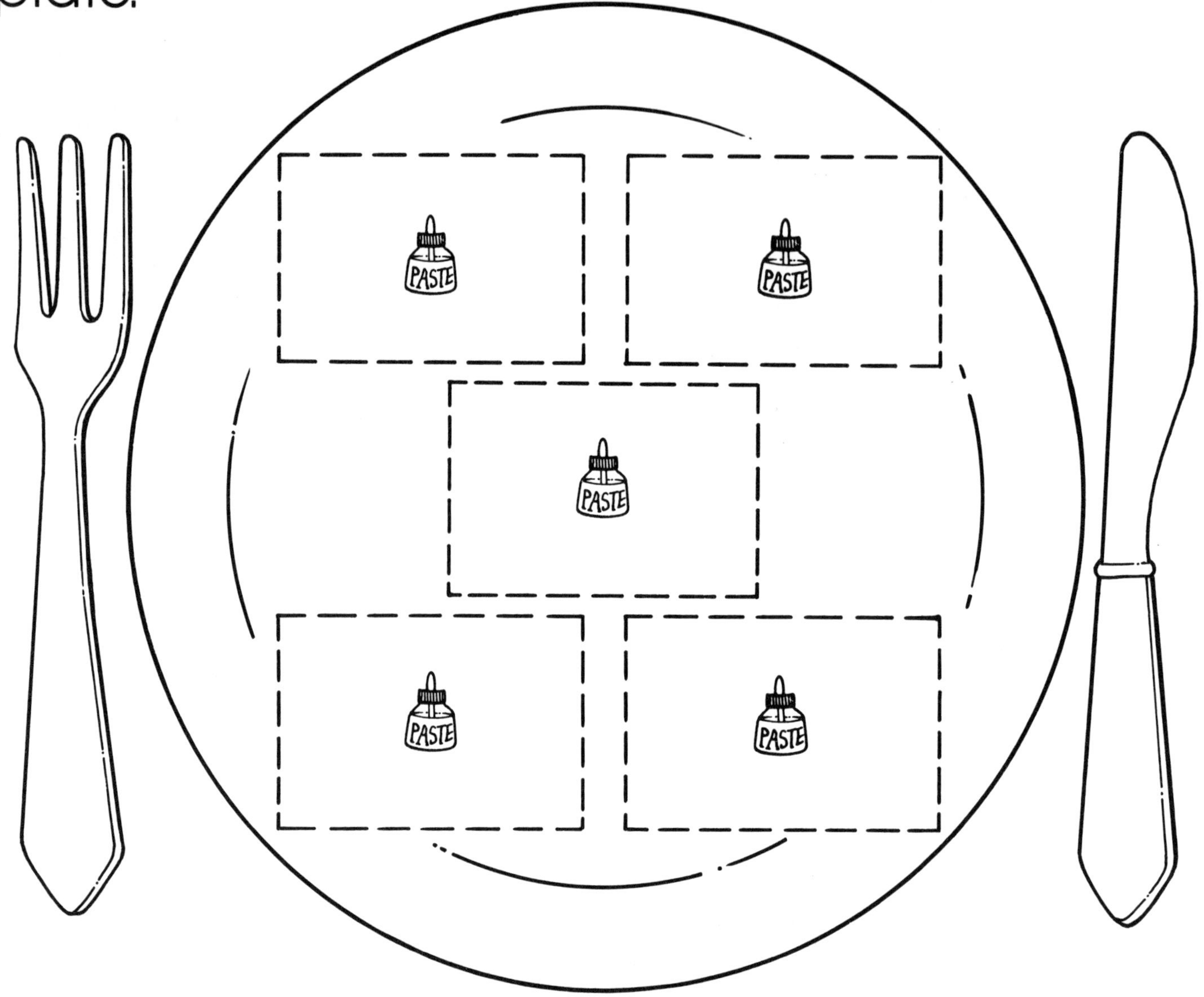

Health

Name _____

🖍 and 🖍 each child who is staying healthy with exercise.

🖍 yourself in the picture doing your favorite activity for exercise.

Health

Name _____

🖍 a line to each picture that shows how to rest to stay healthy.

Health

Name _____

✏️ a **x** on the children who are wearing the wrong clothes.
🖍 and 🖍 the children who are wearing the right clothes.

Health

Name _____

1-2-3 to put the pictures in each row in order.

Safety Name _____

✏ each ✗ red. ✂ and 🧴 on each picture that is not safe.
✏ each safe picture.

Safety Name _____

✏️ the pictures that are not safe.
✏️ the pictures that are safe.

Kdg. Critical Thinking, Self-Awareness IF8701 © 1992 Instructional Fair, Inc.

Community

Name _____

✏️ a line to match each person and place in your town.

Community   Name _____

✏️ the letter in each ☐ to show which place each picture belongs.

Furry Friends

Terrific Toys

Clothes for Kids

The Big Scoop

Snips

A B C D E

Community   Name _____

✏️ each picture of a helper. ✂️ and  missing part of the picture.

Community   Name _____

✏️ a circle around the librarian. Count each child's books. ✏️ the number in the ☐.

Answer Key

Same – Different   Name _____

✏️ the butterflies: 🦋 – yellow 🦋 – purple

Page 1

Same – Different   Name _____

✏️ the top teddy bear: 1 – brown 2 – red 3 – blue 4 – green 5 – yellow

✏️ this teddy bear to look the same as the top one.

Page 2

Same – Different   Name _____

✂️ and 🍯 the matching kite halves. ✏️ each kite.

Page 3

Same – Different   Name _____

✏️ the first row. ✏️ a line from each ice cream cone to another of the same size. ✏️ it the same colors.

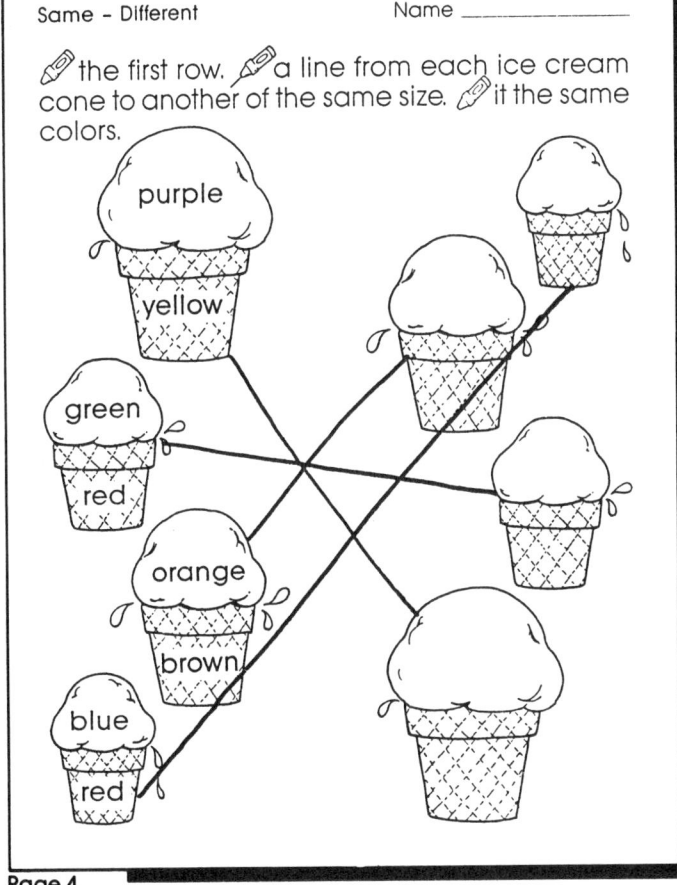

Page 4

Kdg. Critical Thinking, Self-Awareness IF8701   © 1992 Instructional Fair, Inc.

Answer Key

Same - Different   Name _____

✏️ the first picture. 🖌️ a blue circle around 10 things which are different in the second picture.

Page 5

Same - Different   Name _____

✏️ the first picture. ✏️ each picture that is the same as the first one.

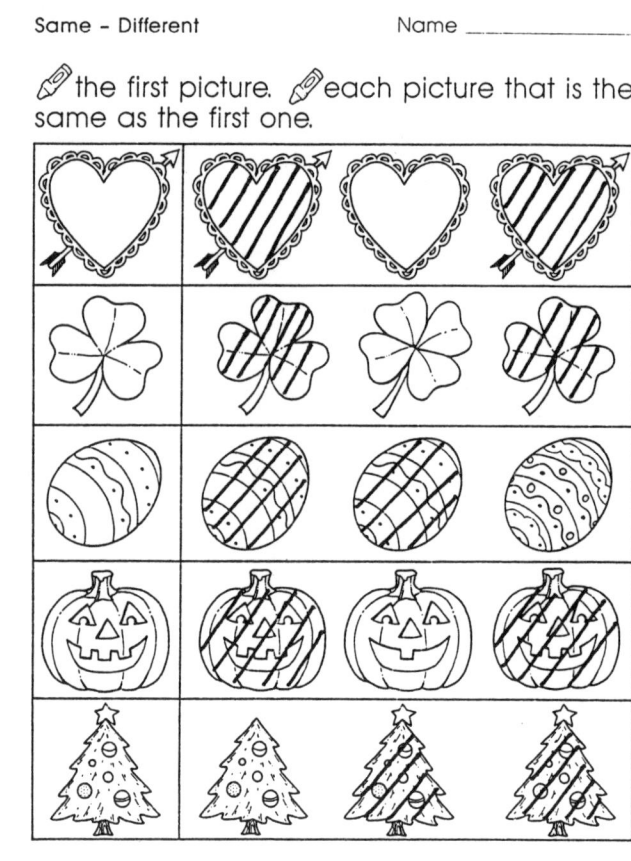

Page 6

Same - Different   Name _____

Look at each group of three things in the picture. 🖍️ a purple X on the one that is different. 🖍️ the other two pictures.

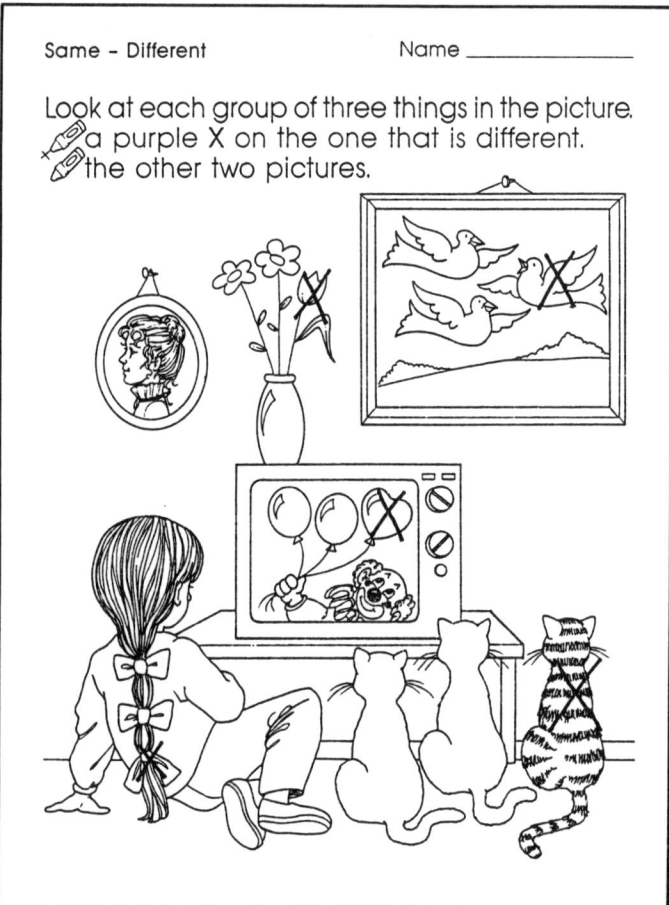

Page 7

Same - Different   Name _____

✏️ the missing parts to make the pictures look the same. ✏️ the pictures with the same colors.

Page 8

Kdg. Critical Thinking, Self-Awareness IF8701   104   © 1992 Instructional Fair, Inc.

Answer Key

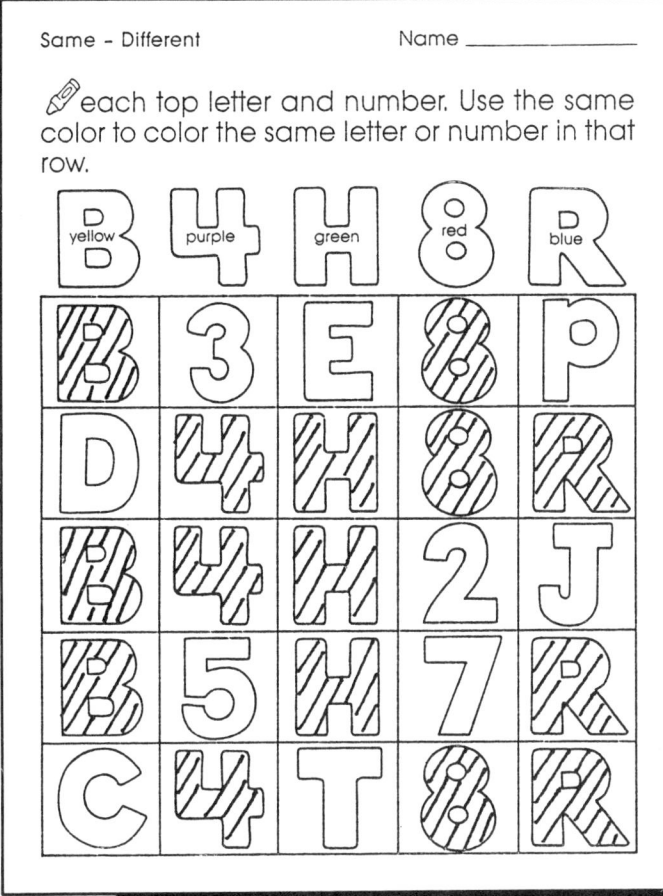

Page 9

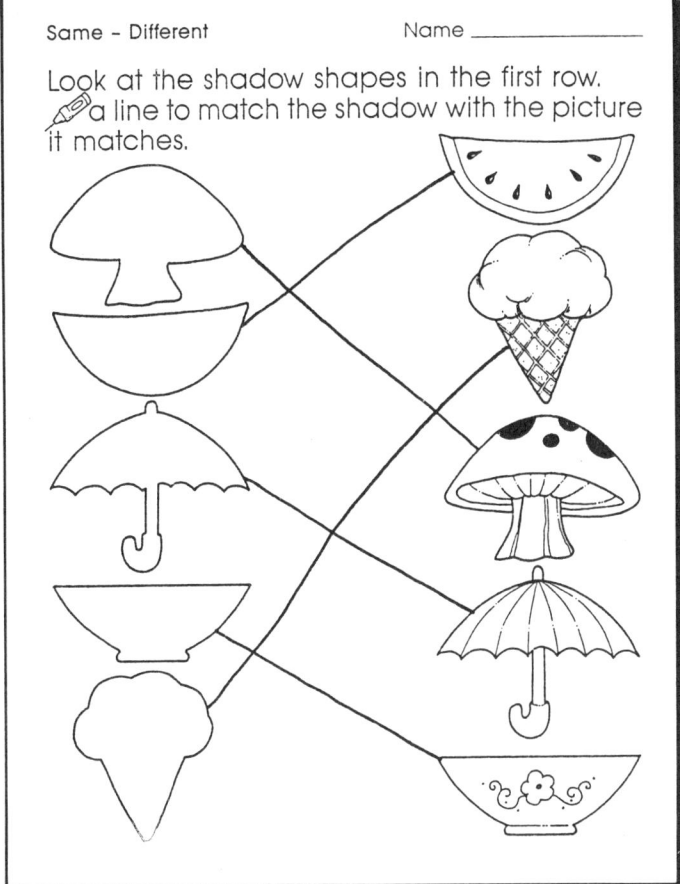

Page 10

Page 11

Page 12

Kdg. Critical Thinking, Self-Awareness IF8701 © 1992 Instructional Fair, Inc.

Answer Key

Page 13

Page 14

Page 15

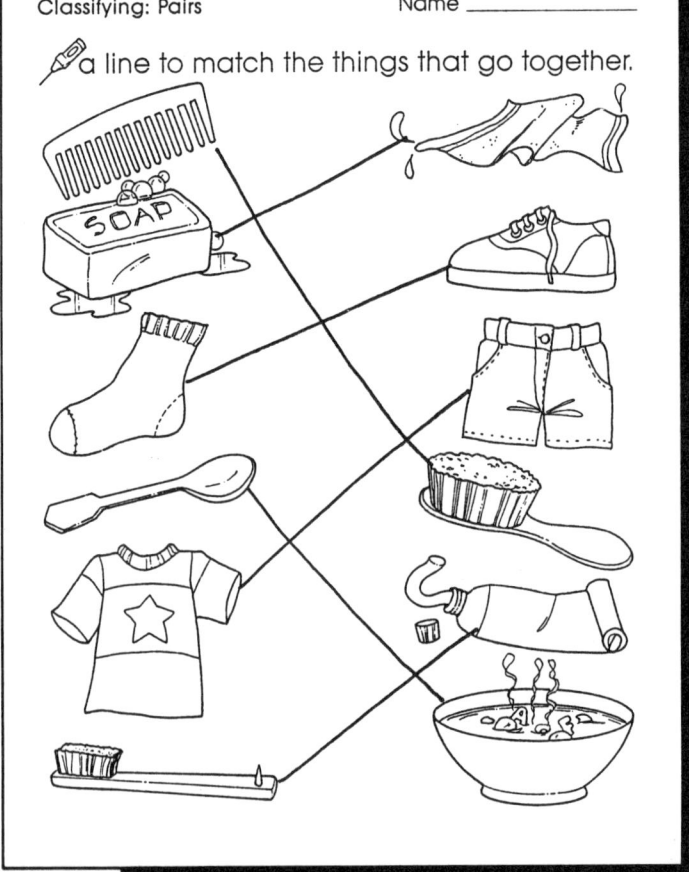

Page 16

Answer Key

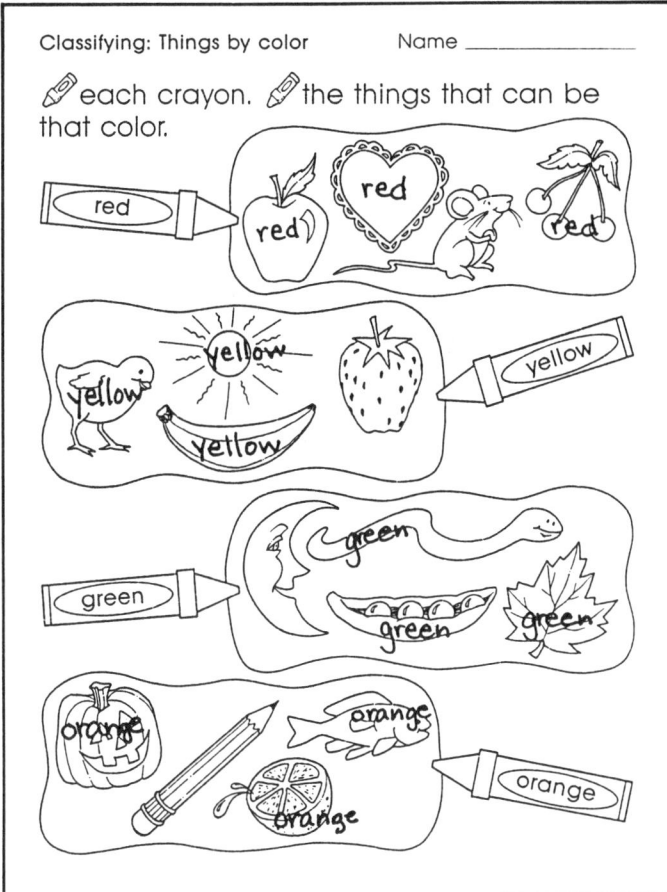

Page 17

Page 18

Page 19

Page 20

Answer Key

Page 21

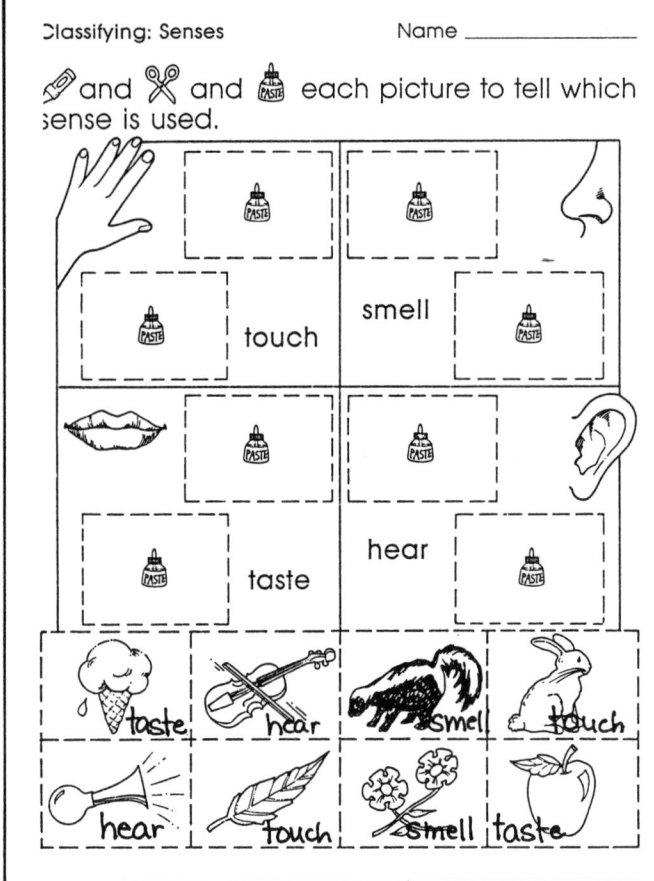

Page 22

Page 23

Page 24

Answer Key

Page 25

Page 26

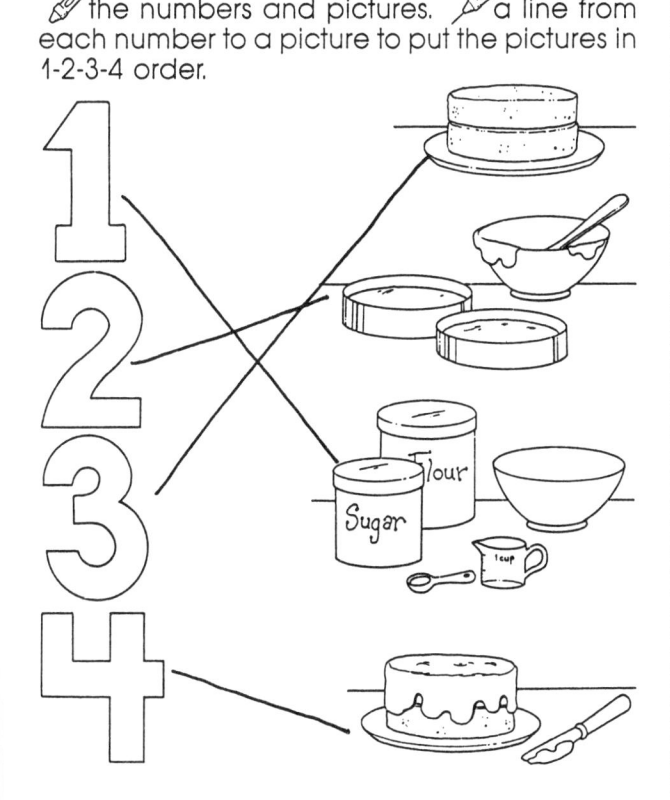

Page 27

Page 28

Answer Key

Answer Key

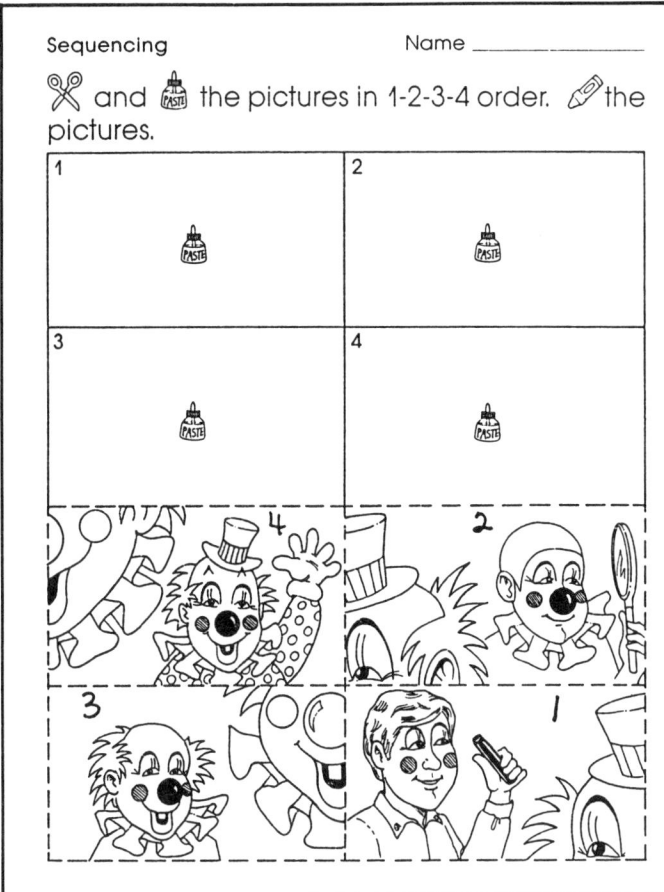

Page 33

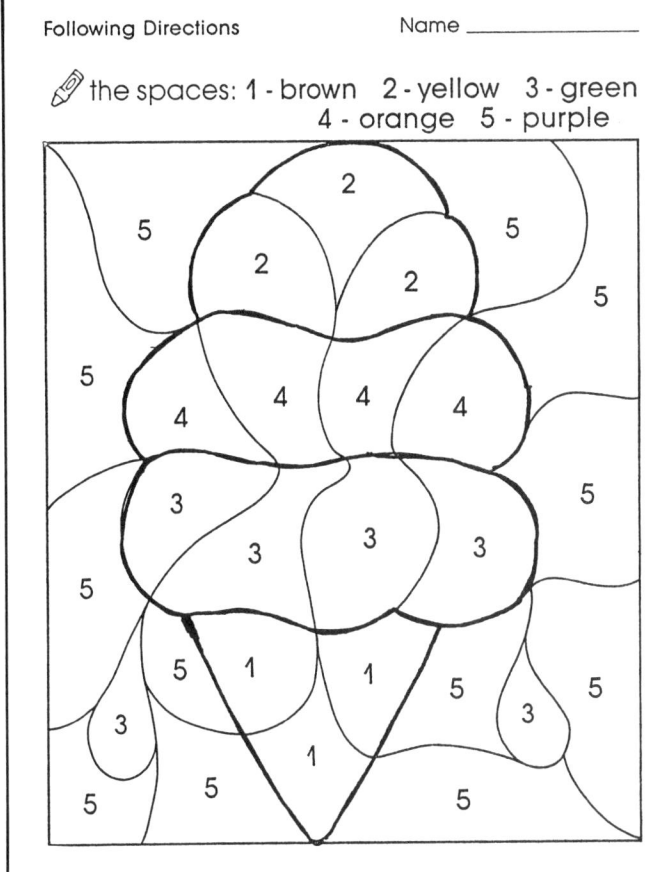

Page 34

Page 35

Page 36

Answer Key

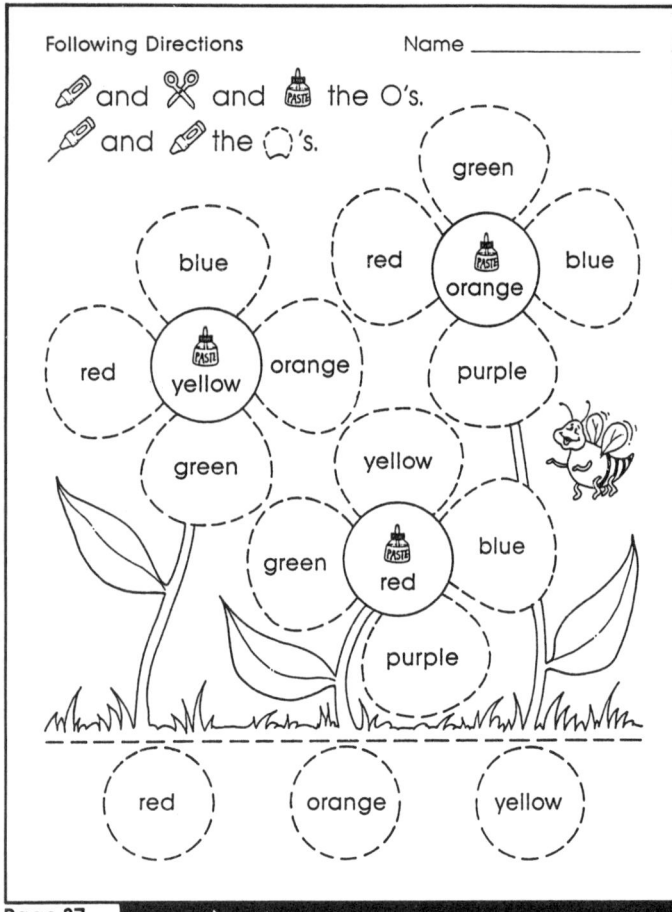

Page 37

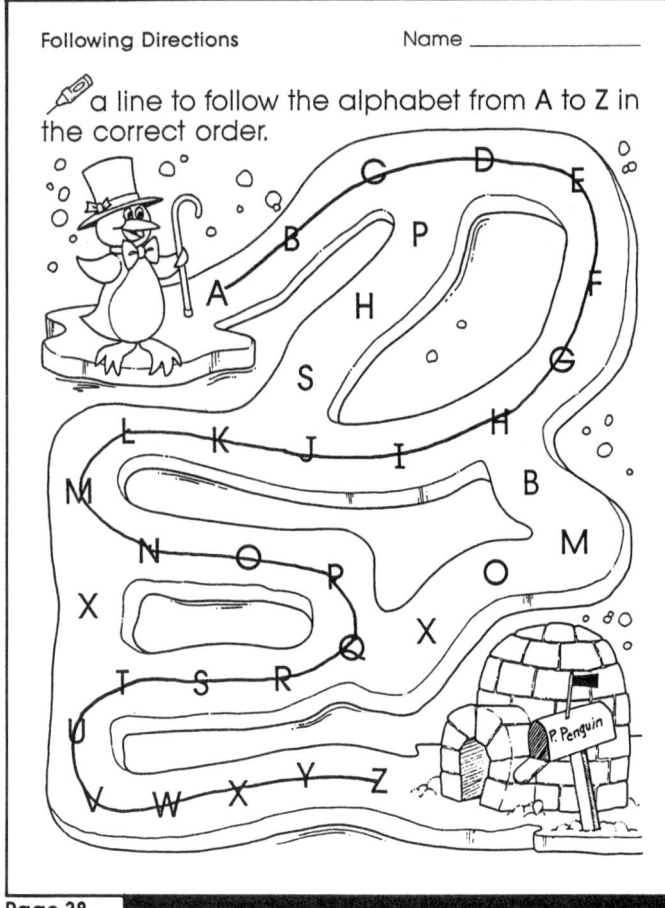

Page 38

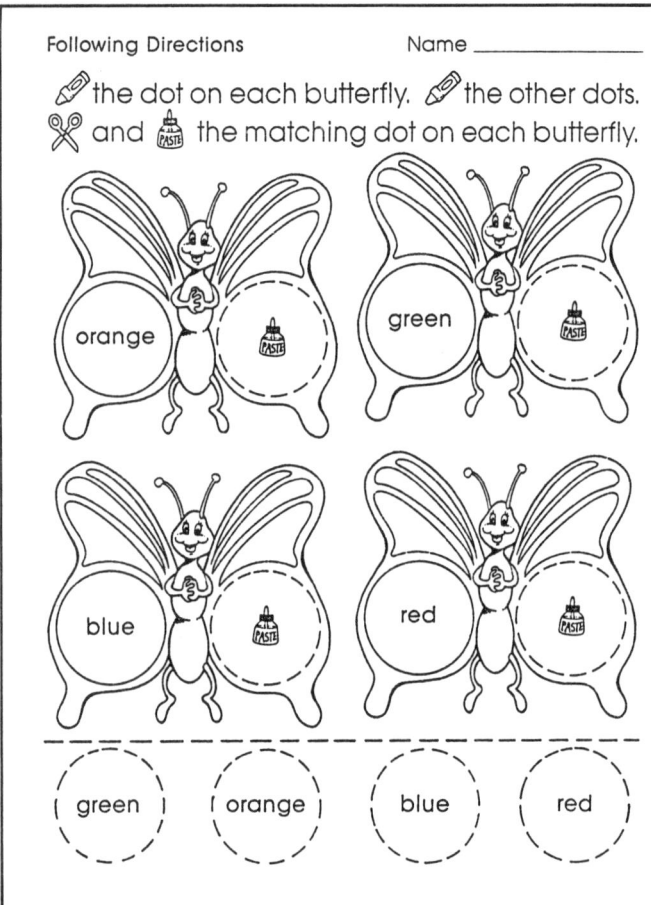

Page 39

Page 40

Answer Key

Page 41

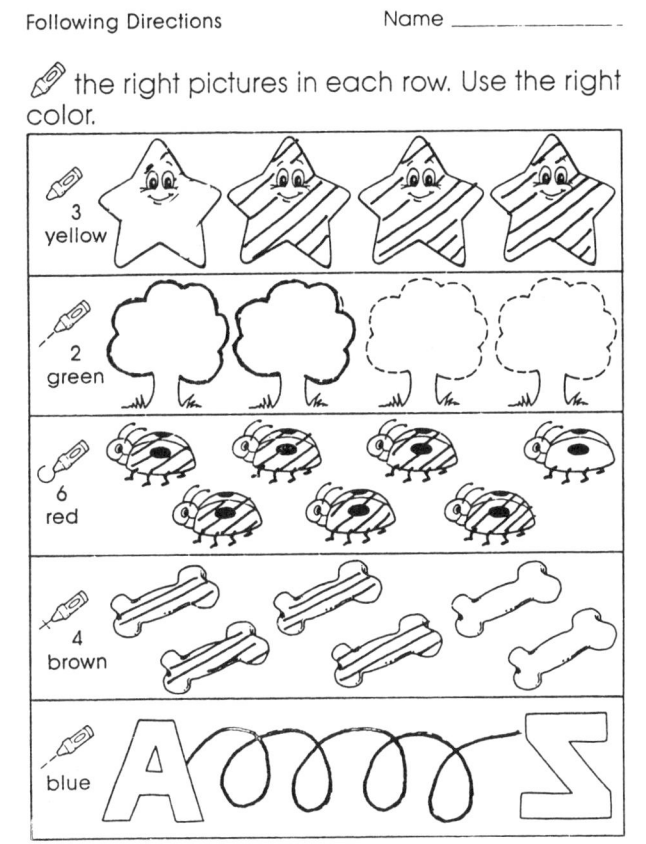

Page 42

Page 43

Page 44

Answer Key

Page 45

Page 46

Page 47

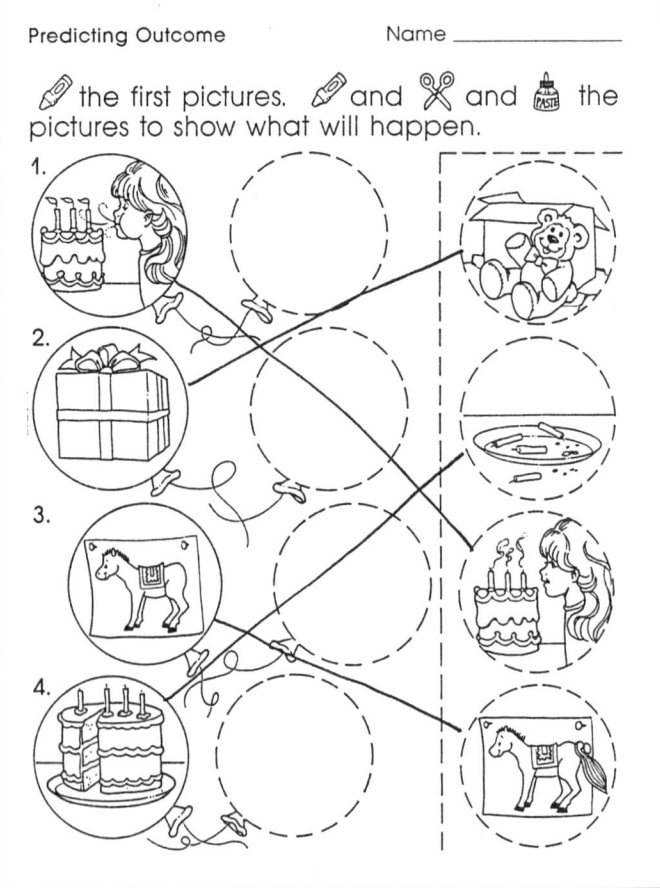

Page 48

Answer Key

Answer Key

Finding Incorrect Concepts Name _____

Help the mother bear find her 5 little bears in the park. ✏️ a red X on the little bears which do not look right. ✏️ the other 5 little bears and ✏️ a line from each to the mother bear.

Page 53

Real and Fantasy Name _____

Look at the picture. ✏️ a purple circle around the 10 things which are make-believe and not real.

Page 54

Self Name _____

✏️ and ✏️ a picture of how you look.

✏️ your name.

Page 55

Self Name _____

✂️ and 🧴 the birthday cake that tells how old you are.
✏️ your age on the balloon.
✏️ and ✏️ a gift in the box that you would like to have.

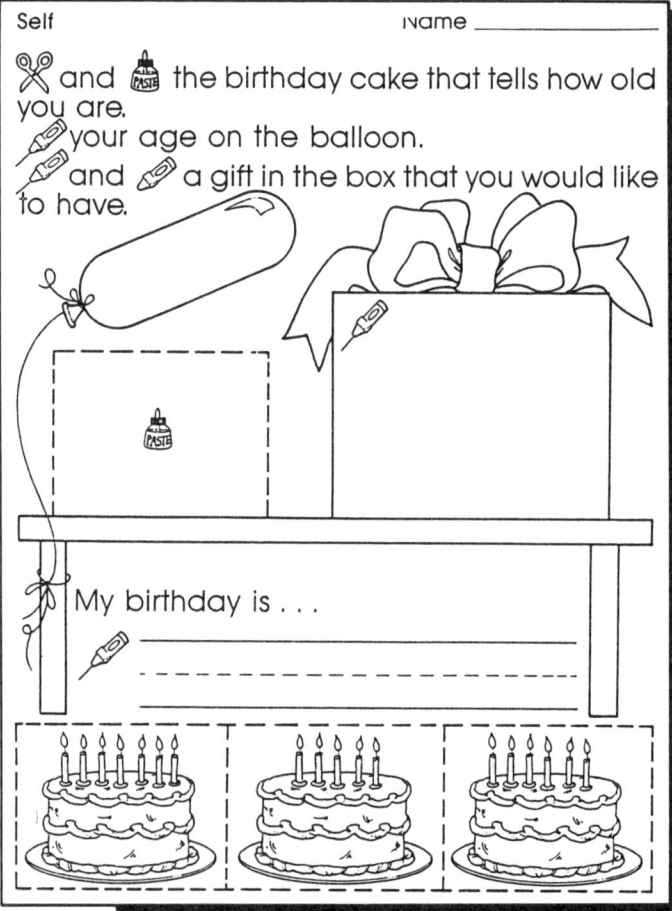

My birthday is . . .

Page 56

Kdg. Critical Thinking, Self-Awareness IF8701   116   © 1992 Instructional Fair, Inc.

Answer Key

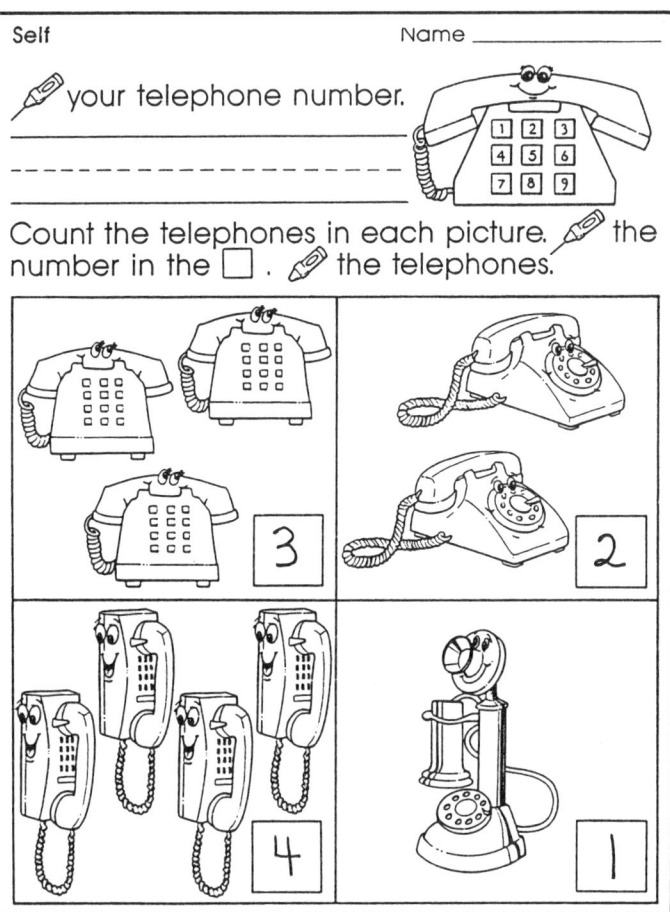

Answer Key

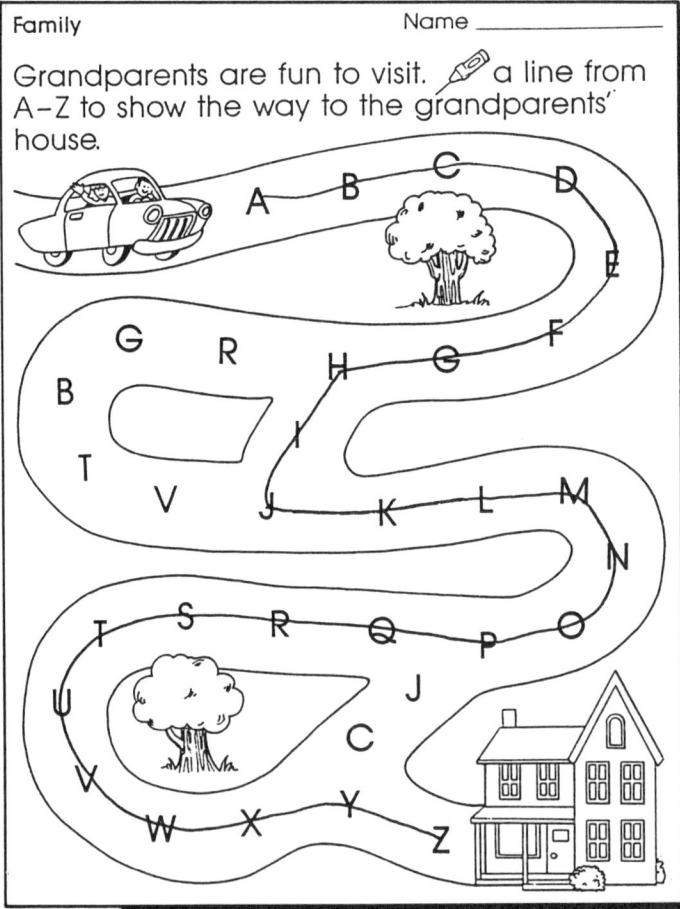

Answer Key

Answer Key

Page 69

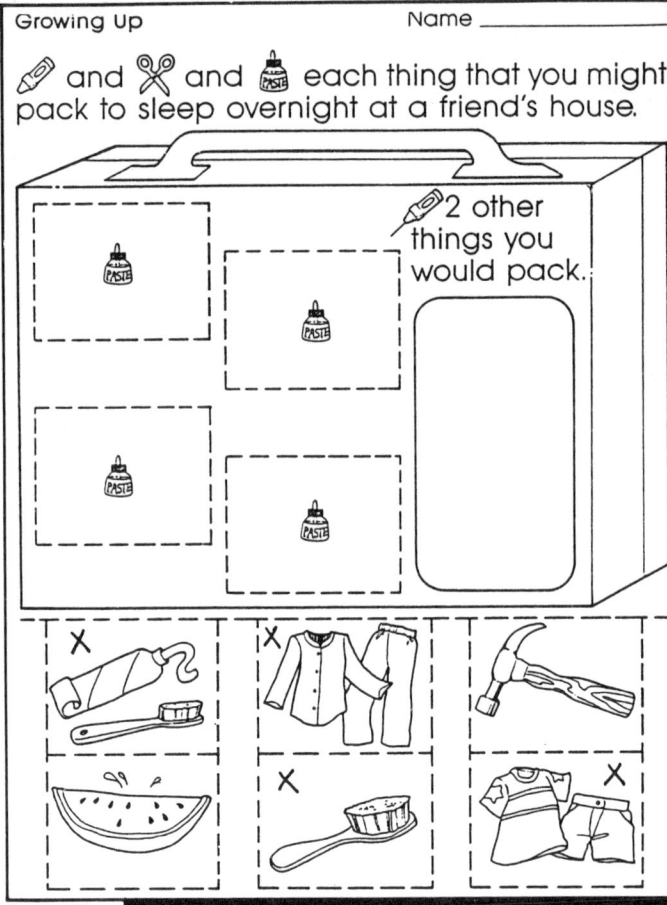

Page 70

Page 71

Page 72

Answer Key

Page 73

Page 74

Page 75

Page 76

Answer Key

School   Name _____

🖍 1-2-3-4 in each ◯ to put the dream in order.

Page 77

School   Name _____

🖍 a circle around the teacher in each picture.
🖍 your three favorite pictures to show how your teacher cares.

Page 78

School   Name _____

🖍 an x on each thing that does not belong on the playground.

🖍 yourself enjoying your favorite activity.

Page 79

School   Name _____

Which pictures show things you can do at school? 🖍 each 🍎 red if it has a school picture.

🖍 the pictures of your favorite school activities.

Page 80

Kdg. Critical Thinking, Self-Awareness IF8701   122   © 1992 Instructional Fair, Inc.

Answer Key

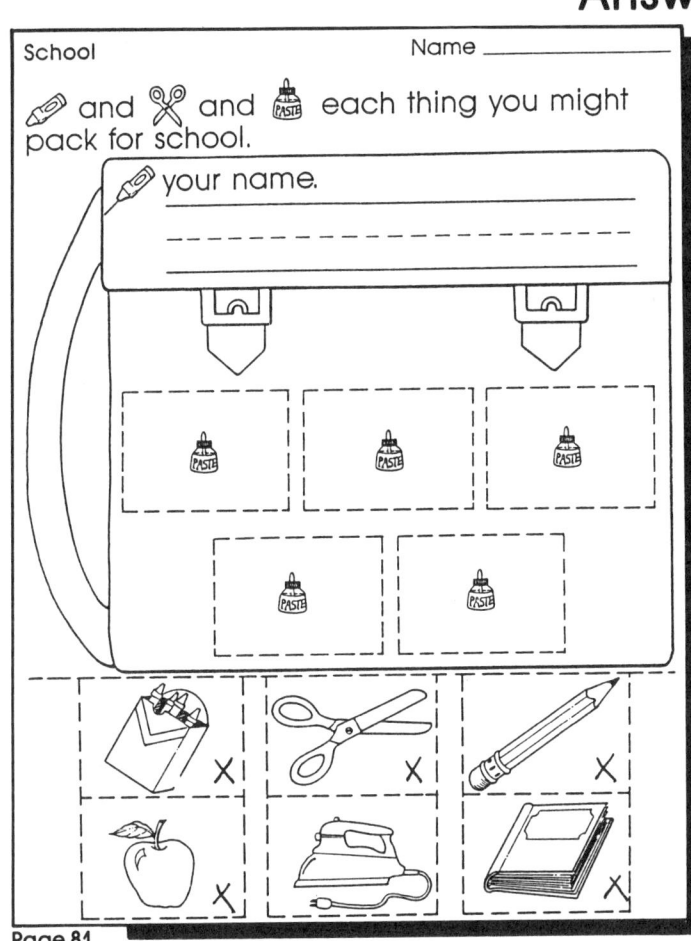

Answer Key

Page 85

Page 86

Page 87

Page 88

Answer Key

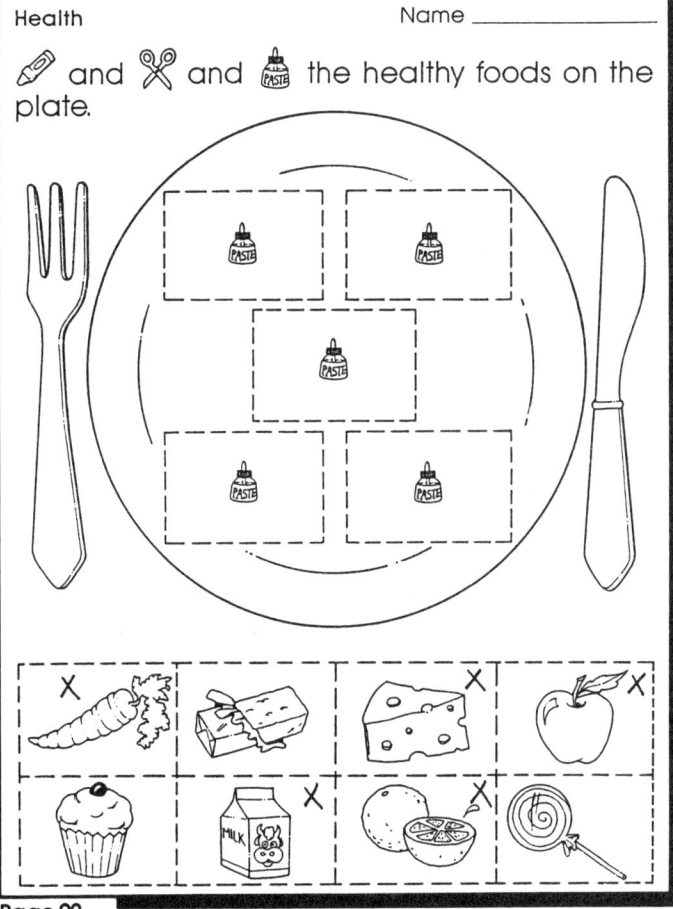

Answer Key

Page 93

Page 94

Page 95

Page 96

Answer Key

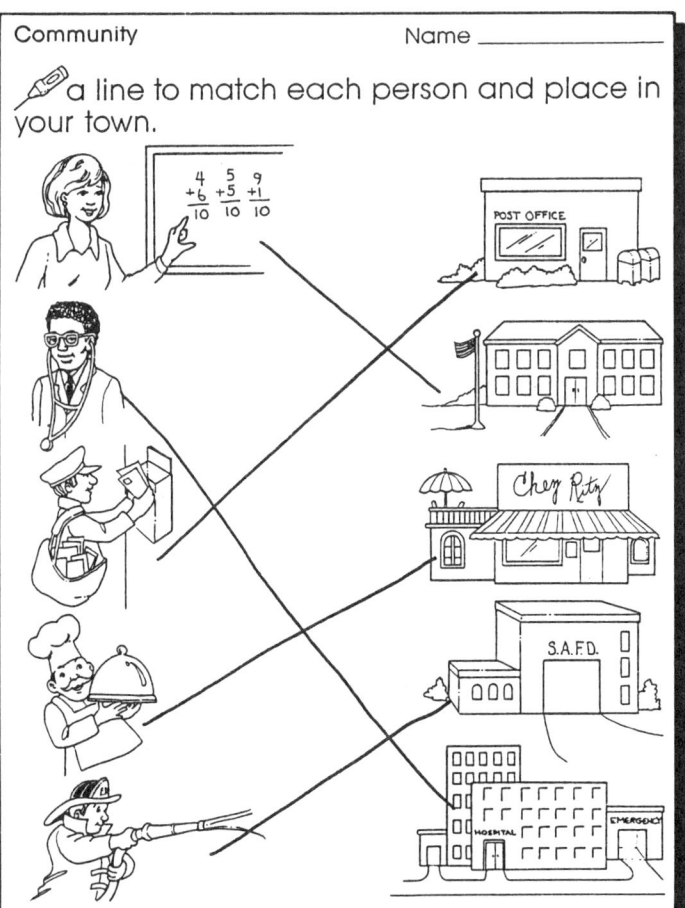

Answer Key

Page 101

Page 102

About the book...
Using delightful, fun illustrations, the activities in this book provide excellent practice with skills such as: same/different, left/right, classifying, following directions, etc. The book also examines self-awareness, beginning with self and family, moving on to school environment, and then to the community.

About the author...
Holly Fitzgerald's special expertise in all areas of Language Arts has been gained over many years of varied teaching experiences at the elementary level. She holds a Master's Degree in Education from Vanderbilt University.

Credits...
Author: Holly Fitzgerald
Editor: Lee Quackenbush
Artist: Carol Tiernon
Production: Pat Geasler
Cover Photo: Frank Pieroni
Cover Design: Jan Vonk